Brian Morton was born in Paisley and grew up in New Orleans-on-Clyde, aka Dunoon, where he acquired a lifelong passion for jazz. He taught at university before spending ten years working on *The Times* and its supplements; he then became a freelance writer and broadcaster, and has had an illustrious career as an arts and music commentator on BBC Radio Scotland and on BBC Radio 3. His publications include *The Penguin Guide To Jazz* which he co-authors with Richard Cook.

PRINCE
A THIEF IN THE TEMPLE

Brian Morton

CANONGATE

Edinburgh · New York · Melbourne

This edition first published in 2007 by
Canongate Books Ltd, 14 High Street,
Edinburgh EH1 1TE

1

British Library Cataloguing-in-Publication Data
A catalogue record for this book is available on
request from the British Library.

978 1 84195 896 5 (13-digit ISBN)
1 84195 896 4 (10-digit ISBN)

Typeset by Palimpsest Book Production Ltd,
Grangemouth, Stirlingshire

Printed and bound in Great Britain by
Creative Print and Design, Ebbw Vale, Wales

www.canongate.net

Sarah, for you . . .
. . . and for the little prince.

Acknowledgements

In a story so much concerned with rumour, counter-rumour, carefuly confected legend, fallings-out, gagging clauses and plain nonsense, who to believe? Almost every detail of Prince's childhood and early years is rebutted or contradicted somewhere in the record. Almost everything that happened later is the subject of endless speculation in an internet community whose size and passion is the best evidence of Prince's artistic longevity. Special thanks to all those imaginatively handled visitors to chat-rooms and message boards, but also to those who've written about Prince before me, and particularly Barney Hoskyns and Dave Hill, whose books *Imp of the Perverse* and *A Pop Life* offered a useful confirmation at a later stage of writing that I wasn't wildly off the mark. Thanks to Arthur Geffen, my virtual guide to Minneapolis, who could have been appalled to know what he was guiding me towards; to the late Colin Smith; to Robert Palmer, Mica Paris, Andrew Pothecary, Cindy Revell; to Jamie Byng, Andy Miller, Helen Bleck and Alison Rae of

Canongate Books, who put up with long delays during the unhappy period after I left the BBC and changed my name to an unpronounceable squiggle and my writing style to an unreadable scrawl; to the members and ex-members of the Prince entourage who spoke (mostly) off the record but with more obvious affection and admiration than malice, and who are paraphrased rather than quoted anonymously in what follows. Thanks above all to Sarah – 'The Most Beautiful Girl in the World' – for putting up with endless plays of endless Prince albums, singles and bootlegs, and for being there during the SLAVE/squiggle days. And to Prince, who I met once semi-officially and from whom I got not one word of sense, except a shared admiration for Miles Davis.

Introduction

The story of Prince – like those of his friend and collaborator Miles Davis, and his fellow Minnesotan Bob Dylan – confirms the falsehood of F. Scott Fitzgerald's famous line about there being no second acts in American lives. The myth of America is all about successive rebirth, about self-determination, about putting time into reverse and seeming to grow younger rather than older. If America is also a language experiment, then archetypal Americans – and Prince, Miles, Dylan inhabit that category – almost always take a playfully cavalier attitude to their own creations.

It's about time, in both the word's senses. If Dylan can take a cherished song and put it to a reggae beat or slow it down so drastically that only a few stray lyrics seem familiar; if Miles could turn his back – as he notoriously used to do on stage – on his own part in some of the classic jazz albums and in favour of youthful street music; then Prince has followed them in treating his own astonishing body of songs – many hundreds in the public domain, countless others as yet unheard – as if they were counters on an improvisational game-field, part of an open flow of 'work' rather than canonical 'works'. The hard thing for any student of Prince, but an endless source of delight and discovery for his admirers, is that the real work does not come through to us as settled 'product' but as a tricksterish chase after bootlegs, reworked ideas, wilful suppressions and mere rumour. It has kept him, depending on how you look at it, either ahead of everyone else, or in sole charge of his own enigmatic game.

The time frame is important. As a very young man, Prince appeared to be the most exciting musician in America, uniquely allowed by a major corporation to make his own music exactly as he chose. Not much more than a decade later, Prince – or whatever he then called himself – was a laughing-stock, paranoid, conspiratorial, creatively burned out, broke. It's hard to judge whether his disappearance from the scene was a personal crisis like the drug-fuelled disillusion that drove Miles Davis away from active music-making at the end of the 1970s or was part of a capriciously contrived withdrawal like Bob Dylan's much exaggerated motorcycle accident. Whatever the truth, all three men came back, Miles and Dylan with something new in their music, Prince seemingly content to catch up with some of the unexplored dimensions of his own almost absurdly eclectic past where a single record might contain elements of jazz, funk, r'n'b, bubblegum pop, psychedelia and hard rock.

The comeback wasn't quite overnight. Prince signalled his intention to be part of the new millennium with 2001's jazz-inflected *Rainbow Children*, which seemed to be largely concerned with his becoming a Jehovah's Witness. Two years later, and this time on the nomadic NPG imprint which allowed him to preserve some degree of creative if not distributional independence, he released *N.E.W.S.*, a set of rough jams that didn't sound like a finished record at all. A year further on, though, an artist who had seemed creatively and commercially down and out was again the biggest gross earner in the music business. Neither 2004's *Musicology* nor 2006's *3121*, his first album for Universal, were anything other than professional, generic Prince records. He seemed to have defied an iron law and to have cheated time. Pushing fifty, Prince had renewed himself.

He's always talked about in terms of a *Zeitgeist*, one which he either expressed to perfection or actually created and inhabited alone. Prince is often spoken of as an enigma, which is rarely a helpful designation. There is, though, a paradox at the heart of his work and reputation. Recent commercial recognition might suggest that Prince was ahead of his time and the market has only now caught up. Prince, though, enjoyed enormous commercial success when still very young – 1984's *Purple Rain* is an industry benchmark – and was only critically marginalised when his behaviour and his music became erratic in the latter part of the decade. He enjoyed greater freedom than any comparable artist in the corporate system and yet presented himself as a 'SLAVE', another African-American whose creative identity was in thrall to the system. He seems to represent a definite moment in cultural time, and yet when one thinks of 1978 or 1979 or the turn into the following decade, it isn't Prince who sums up those years and it isn't Prince who has left a host of successors. For all its apparent attachment to a supposed cusp in American popular culture, Prince's work is about itself, driven by its own rules, prodigal enough to seem even more expansive than it actually was.

To adapt the James Thurber cartoon: what did Prince want to be enigmatic for? The answer is that it was very good for business. He chose his collaborators carefully, didn't always treat them with gratitude but almost always with an element of paranoia; he understood the music business brilliantly – and particularly the importance of publishing, the main term of his 'enslavement' – but at the price of having always to work outside its mainstream. In this regard, he more closely resembles a jazz musician, for whom a measure of marginality is almost inevitable given the imperatives of the culture and the nature of improvisation, and he most closely resembles the older Miles Davis with whom he had a brief on-off friendship and collaboration after Miles's return to performance in the 1980s. Working with his own capriciously evolving circle of collaborators – recruits from the classical world and from Stevie Wonder's band, influences as far apart as Stockhausen and hip-hop – the trumpeter had enjoyed huge commercial success, but at the same cost. The price of creative independence is a certain distance from the mainstream. Unquestionably Prince learned from Miles Davis's example and brokered a unique position for an African-American artist. He made, lost and remade a fortune by giving the public exactly what it wanted, while pretending to refuse such accommodation. For a black man in America, it was a subtle and risky strategem.

Prince's second act was arguably an anticlimax but it was no longer the farce that had fallen in between. Every stage of the Prince story fascinates. Nothing is ever quite clear. Every emphasis seems to entail its opposite. Story-telling is as important as the details of the narrative.

1

London, 1988, and the auditorium of an old theatre, not quite West End, not yet sleazy. It's not the obvious setting for a rock concert and unusually the curtains are down. The audience feel uncomfortably like voyeurs. From behind the red plush curtains, a deep carnal throb. Then a dark slit opens up, its edges lit from behind, crimsoned in excitement. Caught in the same rear spotlight, a tiny figure in purple, improbable clash of colours, unmistakably raw symbolism. Not dancing, not running, but *sprinting* in place; head forward, legs flashing out behind, high-heeled boots like satyr's hooves pounding the stage; face caught in an expression that could be lust, fear, anger, delight, or all of them. Tantrum child and exhibitionist: *Look at me, Dad! . . . Mom!*

For a heart-racing minute the beat and the volume increase. And then someone steps out from the shadows and hands him an instrument that seems to sum up every Cultural Studies module on 'The electric guitar as phallus', except that this one seems also to represent a question mark, an infinity sign and the astrological symbols for male and female. The curtains swing fully back and the lights plunge and sweep over a stage littered with keyboards, drum risers and propped guitars. There are other musicians on the stage, looking momentarily startled, like tomb-raiders caught in a burst of sunlight.

* * *

Seven years earlier, in the *New York Times* of December 10, 1981, the critic Robert Palmer had published a story headed 'Is Prince Leading Music to a True Biracism?' Questions in *NYT* headlines are invariably rhetorical. In the article itself, Palmer rather more carefully voiced the growing consensus that a twenty-three-year-old from Minneapolis – not a moving and shaking town in music terms – had overturned a basic industry nostrum about audience colour, and in the process answered the old question about how to take the black and white out of popular music without leaving it grey or beige. In three albums, or rather in the third of his three albums to date, Prince had restarted the faltering progress of black rock.

His own sense of history is impressive, not just because he claims a prominent place in it but also because he displays an eclectic knowledge of what went before. On that night in London, more than half a controversial decade after Palmer's essay, words like 'protean' and 'mercurial' seemed insufficient.

* * *

It's unusual to see closed curtains at a rock concert, but Prince has always occupied the place where music blurs into theatre and theatre blurs into exhibitionism. In that sense, he is the heir of Little Richard, whose piled-up hair, gigolo moustache and falsetto shrieks resurfaced in Prince. Perhaps only Madonna has pushed harder the idea of pop as illicit spectacle.

Indeed, she was to follow him to London on an earlier visit in 1984. He was touring *Purple Rain*, a quasi-autobiographical album-cum-movie soundtrack that was eventually to shift 13 million copies. The fact that his break-through album was tied in to a certain mythology about his upbringing and emergence in Minneapolis was deeply significant. The movie is an adolescent wish-fantasy. What makes it different and clever is the way Prince and director Albert Magnoli manage to weave together themes of display, abandon, secrecy and forbidden longing with cross-threads of responsibility, guilt and self-control. The Kid's motorcycle is laughably phallic, but doesn't he ride it with impressive care and road sense? And isn't there something unexpectedly tender, almost husbandly, about his seductions?

* * *

There was nothing remotely uxorious about his horny, blatant onstage persona, which had moved on from the black panties, boots and bandanna phase, but in 1988 still hadn't quite yet reached the stage where Prince disported on a heart-shaped bed with one of his dancers. Fans of Prince have a tendency to conflate many concert appearances into one climactic gig. In the same way, Miles Davis's comeback tours in the 1980s – equally spectacular in the wardrobe department, though inevitably cooler in demeanour – all seem to blend together into one continuous performance.

I have false memories of that first gig, which has become a kind of composite. Clothes, songs and other guitars from earlier and later in Prince's career seem to be part of it. The curtain wasn't sensuous velvet, but an ordinary fire-curtain pressed into dramatic service. The supporting personnel shifts, combining the adolescent-male pack behaviour of the early groups with the weird mix of exploitation and feminism of later line-ups; like singer Robert Palmer, Prince was capable of presenting women as cloned sex-objects, but he also operated an impressive gender democracy, giving the likes of Wendy Melvoin and Lisa Coleman a prominent role in the Revolution group and putting his production and songwriting weight behind a whole series of female acts. Again, much like Miles Davis's last decade, conscious, fact-checked memory will yield one set of impressions (mostly of impressive band members and evolving repertoire) while a more primitive recall narrows the focus to just the leader and what appears to be a single, ongoing, history-of-black-music guitar solo.

* * *

The other word, after 'protean' and 'mercurial', routinely applied to Prince is 'seminal'. Ever a man to push his metaphors with excessive literalism, Prince used to feign ejaculation over the first few rows, jerking a milky liquid from the neck of his guitar. (I have no false memory of being so showered, and would seek immediate counselling if I had.) What does come back is how aggressively Prince had plundered the tombs and temples of American music, and how adroitly he personalised the masks and trappings. And how comically: if subsequent chapters fail to deliver a convincing account of the humour in Prince's art, that's because it is so wryly and ironically embedded in otherwise serious things.

He'd been widely touted as the reincarnation of Jimi Hendrix. In reality, Prince's guitar style has little to do with the blues and owes far more to the sustained, almost mystical tonality of Carlos Santana. He was eager to oblige, though, playing behind his head and picking strings with those strange pointy teeth he prefers to keep hidden during interviews. There were subtler echoes, not least that just about every song turned into a long, loose, electronic jam, but turning his back on the audience for long minutes seemed an echo of Miles Davis's most ambiguous gesture, which some said was contempt for whitey, others claimed was a sign of his concentration and empathy with the band. In Prince's case, it may have been no more than a tease, a way of showing off his ass, but he knew where it had come from. Prince deeply admired Miles's working methods – taping hours of 'rehearsal' in a bid to push himself and his fellow musicians beyond comfortably familiar idioms – and often alluded to the trumpeter's phenomenal workrate as a model for his own hyperactivity. As Prince left the stage, the band played a rocked-up version of the bebop classic 'Now's The Time', by Miles's one-time employer Charlie Parker, whose shambolic lifestyle masked and eventually foreshortened a brilliantly intuitive talent. Prince reportedly still keeps photographs of both men on his desk at Paisley Park.

That night in 1988 Prince duck-walked like T-Bone Walker and Chuck Berry, wailed righteously like Little Willie John, mugged and flounced like Little Richard. One minute he was stock-still, hypnotised by a version of Stevie Wonder's lateral jazz-soul; the next he was doing endless splits to a relentless funk groove that even James Brown and the JBs would have felt had been taken too far. He sang an intense gospelly song that inescapably recalled Al Green, who took very literally black soul's sometimes easy, sometimes contradictory blend of sacred and profane by becoming a church minister (albeit a minister who cheerfully ogles pretty girls during his warm-up addresses). British audiences wouldn't have been so quick to spot references in the stage act to Rick James's marriage of soul and live sex show; James, with whom Prince toured in 1979, never really made it this side of the Atlantic. They would, though, have recognised the debt to Sly and the Family Stone, primed by the shared vocals of '1999' (one of his first British hits), by a slew of references in the *Purple Rain* movie, and by the faux-illiterate spelling of songs. In 1970, Sly had released 'Thank You (Falettinme Be Mice Elf Agin)' with a Larry Graham bass groove that influenced everyone from Prince to Michael Jackson. Though Prince stopped short of calling his first album *4 U* he'd adopted the street shorthand style, which in those days came from graffiti and school slambooks rather than phone-texting. As well as 4/fors and U/yous, his liner notes were littered with eye/I graphics, hearts and squiggles, something he'd done since schooldays. It wasn't to be very long before he adopted an unpronounceable squiggle as his name.

What complicated Prince's clever referencing of black music and prompted journalist Robert Palmer's rhetorical headline was his parallel interest in white rock and white songwriters. There was a working assumption in the industry that black musicians didn't – or couldn't – rock, and neither did black audiences; r'n'b, soul, funk, perhaps a leaven of jazz, but a fundamental resistance to the basic backbeat of rock'n'roll. There were other, concurrent efforts to inject some life into what sprouted capital letters as Black Rock (notably Vernon Reid's Living Color) but it was Prince who smudged the distinction and desegregated pop demographics. Jimi Hendrix had shown the way in some regards (and was Reid's role model) and, of course, Michael Jackson's *Thriller* had attracted huge sales with an audience who didn't usually buy r'n'b.

Hendrix's and Jackson's success were to some degree accidents of musical history. Jimi's style, stagecraft, and eager recolonisation of white blues rock came to notice first of all in Britain; the Experience trio was two-thirds white and they had a white manager. In a somewhat different way, *Thriller* filled what seemed like a creative vacuum in pop music, left since Stevie Wonder's muse deserted him. What made Prince different was that he was also able to write and play convincingly colour-blind music. Long before the well-crafted psychedelia of *Raspberry Beret*, Prince was in thrall to The Beatles. He could also windmill and crash out power chords like Pete Townshend of The Who, and one of the unexpected influences of his teenage years in Minneapolis had been the 'bicep rock' of Grand Funk Railroad, still possibly the noisiest band ever.

Onstage, Prince didn't have quite the range of vocal styles available to him in the studio, but a clear and steady falsetto was one of them and, though it made reference to the peer-less Curtis Mayfield, there was no mistaking in it an unlikely debt to Joni Mitchell, especially the laid-back mystery and buried tension of *The Hissing of Summer Lawns*. It's an influence that can still be heard on 1987's 'Starfish and Coffee' from the brilliant *Sign 'O' The Times* album, but it's pervasive. 'She taught me about colour', he said to a reporter, though in this case at least he meant voice and instrumental colour rather than the industry demographics he was in the process of changing. Elsewhere, he credited Joni with shaping his understanding of space and silence. In turn, Mitchell acknowledged the impact she'd had on him: 'Prince has assimilated some of my harmonies, which because they come out of my guitar tunings, is unusual. A lot of the time my chords depict complex emotions . . .'

* * *

Such eclecticism is not unusual in black music. To some degree, it defines it. So Michael Eric Dyson argues in his book *Between God and Gangsta Rap*, published in 1996, the year Prince's grasp on that rich dichotomy seemed to come temporarily unstuck. To what extent Prince's cherry-picking, not just from within the black tradition but between traditions, was new or merely different in degree is scarcely important. What is beyond doubt is that the music of the 1980s and after would have been radically different without him. His most distinctive albums – *Dirty Mind*, *1999*, *Purple Rain*, *Sign 'O' The Times*, *Emancipation* – are all contemporary classics. Between 1978 and 1988, he matured, not just as a songwriter and musician, but also as an engineer and producer, turning the slightly fussy feel of his first two albums, the antithesis of a home-made, punk aesthetic, into product that major labels and studios couldn't match. At the same time, his vehement reaction to corporate pressure became a model for other musicians stuck with no-win contracts or creatively restricted by the men on the twenty-fifth floor. (He put in a call to George Michael during the British singer's battles with Sony.) Whether Prince really created a new, 'biracial' music or was merely a gifted eclectic, less an innovator than a brilliant assimilator who fashioned his own creative environment by plunder – sometimes rich grave goods, sometimes overlooked shards – remains the question. The background to it, if not quite the answer, lies in Prince's upbringing in a quiet Midwestern city.

2

Minneapolis, 1997. A baby boy is playing in the dirt with a purple ball when his attention is diverted by three gold chains half buried beside him. His cries disturb a television journalist standing nearby to report on the start of a rock tour that is going to reverse 'the low concert grossing of even the biggest of the superstar acts'. The baby jumps into his teenage mother's arms and shows her what he's found. 'The young mother holds the chains to her bosom and begins to remember back, back . . . five years ago.'

* * *

Minneapolis, 1992. Warner Brothers release ⚥, its non-verbal emblem a combination of the astrological signs for male and female. It's the work of the label's most charismatic but also most troublesome artist. The album is supposed to come with a video programme that links sixteen funk songs into a narrative about a rock star and a teenage Egyptian princess. The inheritor of a sacred relic, the 'three gold rings of Turin', she is being pursued by the seven men who murdered her father. In an attempt to find them first, she sends a tape of her dancing to the legendary rock star. He falls in love at once, as princes are supposed to fall in love with princesses. But he fears emotional entrapment and consoles himself in sex with others. In so doing, he also destroys seven older versions of himself who are, of course, the old king's killers. A double destiny is thus enacted. The 320-year-old pretender and the sixteen-year-old princess are mystically united.

The journalist Vanessa Bartholomew was played in the video by Kirstie Alley, who made her name in the cult television series *Cheers*. Her part was largely cut out of the final album mix. It survives in a short abortive conversation with the star – he hangs up as soon as she admits the conversation is being taped – and in her later attempt to question him about about a rumour that the crown princess of Egypt has become a member of his band, the New Power Generation. He flirts with her, pretends to be called Victor, and hangs up mid-sentence. The princess, for whom the whole elaborate story was confected, was played by a dancer-singer called Mayte. The rock star was, for now, still known as Prince.

Their mystical union was made flesh almost five years later and almost at the date imagined in the ♀ video. On February 14, 1996, Prince and Mayte Janelle Garcia exchanged vows at a church in Minneapolis. It was a complex time career-wise for the musician. Over the

previous year, he'd taken to appearing in public, most notoriously at the Brits Music Awards, with the word SLAVE
written in eyebrow pencil on his cheek. (So iconic a moment
was this that some time later a member of Blur appeared
at the same event with DAVE pencilled on his cheek.) At the
start of 1996, Prince had parted company with his enslavers
Warner Brothers, the record company which had made him
a star with unprecedented control over his own music, by
dashing off in just ten days a contract-fulfilling final album
before he launched his own NPG imprint on EMI. Slight
it may have been, but that year's well-named *Chaos and
Disorder* still sold substantially better than Mayte's own
Children of the Sun album, a solo project written and
produced by Prince.

In November 1996, just before the launch of a triple set
significantly called *Emancipation*, Mayte gave birth to a
premature baby boy. Gregory was fated never to find gold
chains in the dust. The infant was diagnosed as having a
medical condition known as acrocephalosyndactyly, more
commonly as Pfeiffer's syndrome or 'clover-leaf syndrome'
after a distinctive deformation of the skull. In what has to
be seen as an emancipation for a child fated never to see,
hear, taste or smile, the boy died a fortnight later, after his
life support system was switched off. To everyone's astonishment, Prince went ahead with release plans for the new
album, threw a lavish party and fulfilled video and press
commitments. The rumour mill suggested that the baby's
uterine heartbeat could be heard on *Emancipation*. The

rumour mill also picked up on a line in the seemingly auto-biographical 'The Sacrifice of Victor' which suggested Prince had suffered from epilepsy in early childhood. Did this explain his small stature – five foot two to five foot four depending on your source – and did it maybe suggest that Gregory's problems were hereditary? There were more surprises to come. On *Oprah*, he denied that there had been anything wrong with the child. On a slightly later occasion, three weeks after the boy's death, Prince told assembled journalists that he was 'enjoying fatherhood'.

* * *

It may have seemed, and might seem now, just one more self-consciously bizarre pronouncement in a career marked by the most profound self-consciousness imaginable, but there is a recurrent twist to Prince's references to fathers and sons. An Oedipal strain is never far from the surface, and neither is the romantic presumption that the child is wiser than the man.

For much of his career, Prince has played the knowing child-man, and turned that enigmatic image against an industry which began as nurturing and permissive and became increasingly denying and censorious. The loss of Gregory was followed by separation from the label that had launched his career with an unprecedented emancipation from corporate control. If the first album was a joyous whirl in a hand-held spotlight, Warner expected something different of their artist's creative adolescence, and the infamous (though in retrospect rather innocuous) *Black Album* was said to have been made behind closed doors, the musical equivalent of whacking off in the bathroom. Then the sulks and rages, then the inevitable parting.

It's an image reinforced by Prince's diminutive stature, by the fatal glamour of momma's clothes closet, and in the music itself by his addiction to switches and pedals that could switch between a falsetto vocal and a deep parental growl that sounded like the voice of the superego and some-times like God himself. In that abortive interview with Vanessa Bartholomew, Prince explains why he sounds different on the telephone: 'It's a tongue box . . . I use it to disguise my voice.' It was part of his genius to recognise that the voice is the truest self but also the most cunning disguise. Much of his singing in this period is in borrowed voices: camp squeals that might imitate a mother's or a girlfriend's fussing, the soulful bleat of a preacher, a pervert's heavy breathing or the kind of voice that tells you the kid is safe and where to leave the money. Few artists are more instantly recognisable for *not* sounding like themselves. What makes a Prince album distinctive is how the music is put together.

There's a corollary to that in the received view of who and what Prince is. He wouldn't be the first pop star to rewrite his own biography, lie about his age and about his parents; Jim Morrison of The Doors used to pretend that his mother and his father, an admiral in the US Navy, had been killed in a car wreck, when both were inconveniently and bemusedly alive. What's interesting about Prince, as Dave Hill points out in his 1989 biography *Prince: A Pop Life*, is the star's collusion in the lies and fabrications of other people, childhood friends, ex-friends, Minneapolis hangers-on with a hook into a free lunch or a tip-off fee. It seems scarcely to have mattered to Prince whether the invention was his own or not. As in his work, which plunders all up and down the coastline of black American music, he appropriated anything and everything said about him, as if that *was* his reality. 'Image' – that treacherously inclusive word – was less important than the latest carefully confected persona or *alter ego*. It was as if every time he looked in the mirror Prince expected to see someone other than himself and certainly someone who did not remind him of his father.

* * *

For all his fantasies of reincarnation and royal blood, Prince's version of the 'family romance' is relatively modest. It's not unusual for children – and not just self-mythologising rock stars – to imagine that their real parents are dead, or that they are being raised by other than their blood parents, who are, of course, far more high-born and exotic. In the original treatment to the film *Purple Rain*, then simply known as *Dreams*, he explored just such a possibility, but for the moment his self-mythologising took a more modest turn. In February 1981, just after *Controversy* was released, *Rolling Stone* announced that Prince was the son of a half-black father and an Italian mother. It was a genealogy that from the magazine's unshakably white middle-class point of view obviously made some sense of *Controversy*'s new brand of carnal funk and its otherwise indefinable difference from earlier bump-and-grind acts like the Ike and Tina Turner Revue, Millie Jackson or Rick James, for whom Prince was to open on tour that year.

Unfortunately, the lineage was twice wrong. The idea had got around some time previously that Prince was the son of a black *mother* and Italian *father*, and that could be traced back to an interview he gave (when he was still giving interviews) to the *Los Angeles Times*. He'd said that both parents were light-skinned blacks, there was a sprinkle of Italian blood on the paternal side and a poorly researched Native American connection on the maternal. Though common enough, these were important marks of exception, of a potentially exotic lineage, and Prince may well have exaggerated at least one aspect of his descent.

What they *were* was probably less important than *where* they met. Mattie Shaw was a girl from Baton Rouge, Louisiana, who like many before her had left the South in search of whatever version of a better world she dreamed of: less prejudice, brighter lights, greater economic opportunity. Unlike most, drawn to New York City, Detroit,

Chicago, or – the short hop – Washington D.C., Mattie and her sister Edna Mae came to live in Minneapolis, possibly the least black of all the major American cities. There, her singing caught the attention of a local jazz pianist, who asked her to sit in with his group. In June 1956, twenty-two-year-old Mattie became John L. Nelson's second wife; he was a fellow Louisianan and eighteen years her senior. By day John worked for Honeywell Computers. By night, though, he continued to indulge the showbiz side of his nature, an aspect which surfaced whenever in later years he appeared in his son's entourage with ever-younger and more glamorous girlfriends. He was the front man of the 'Prince Rogers Trio'.

Spurious aristocratic titles are part of jazz mythology. Count Basie and Duke Ellington are only the most famous members of a jazz lineage that in places reads like the *Almanach de Gotha*: kings, earls, more dukes and counts, and princes, too. The only difference about this otherwise obscure Minneapolis group, which played mostly lounge gigs, reportedly in the smooth manner of the Ahmad Jamal group, was what it bequeathed to pop history.

At 6.17 p.m. on June 7, 1958, Mattie Shaw Nelson gave birth to a boy at Mount Sinai Hospital in Minneapolis. It was the child's first stroke of luck that his father didn't play with the Swinging Dixie Cups or the Minneapolis Three because John Nelson decided to name his new son after the band. The birth certificate actually gives the child's name as 'Prince Roger Nelson'. It may be that the dropped 's' was deliberate, a concession to Mattie's preference for a more familiar boy's name; a clerk's haste seems equally likely.

Talking to the *Los Angeles Times* in January 1981, he said, 'I think my father was kind of lashing out at my mother when he named me', but typically provided no explanation or context for the remark. John Nelson may have lashed out in other ways as well. If *Purple Rain* is even notionally autobiographical, it was a sometimes violent household. Some of Prince's closest associates have hinted at a history of abuse. The artist himself has remained reticent on the subject, beyond a few rumour-fuelling hints in songs like 'Papa' on the desperate 1994 *Come* album, which includes the unexpectedly naked line 'Don't abuse children or they turn out like me'. There is more of the same on 'The Sacrifice of Victor', the final track on the so-called *Love Symbol Album* (1992), and on 'Da, Da, Da' from *Emancipation* (1996). It requires no great effort to comprehend that this was genuinely an issue for Prince.

It's no more than a happy coincidence that a certain uncertainty and fluidity of names was part of Prince's story from the very start. Later, he tried to abandon the name altogether, overtly to neutralise Warner branding, but maybe to escape his father's embarrassing self-advertisement, or simply because he didn't like it. There was more to it than that, though. The Portuguese poet Fernando Pessoa used umpteen creative personas to express different parts of his creative personality or different creative personalities. Prince can't claim quite as many heteronyms, but he has also worked as Alexander Nevermind, Camille, Joey Coco, Christopher Tracy, Jamie Starr, Tora Tora, Victor and the evil Spooky Electric, disguises which only fooled the uninitiated.

The uninitiated sometimes included childhood friends, sections of the press and of the music business. On the South Side streets and at high school, kids would see him coming and call him 'Princess'. To those tabloids mystified and irritated by the look, the sound and the attention-grabbing antics he became 'Ponce' or, recalling his most celebrated album and film role, 'the Purple Pain'. Perhaps John Nelson was lashing out not at his wife but at the child who would far outstrip his modest fame.

As always with Prince, it's virtually impossible to separate real events from legend, but in Barney Hoskyns's *Imp of the Perverse* there is a small anecdote that adds a convincing detail to the Oedipal drama. Prince recalls sneaking in the back door of a club to watch his father play. He is maybe five years old, certainly no more than nine or ten, standing hidden in a service area, looking at the lights, listening to the jingle of ice in glasses and soft feminine laughter at darkened tables. There he's found by one of the club dancers, a beautiful girl, scantily dressed, on her way outside for a cigarette. Mock-angry and liking his looks and his sass, she takes the boy outside to wait for his father. Maybe she flirts with him and he precociously flirts back. There might even be a kiss on his cheek or, to embarrass him, on the mouth. Even if it's invented rather than a genuine primal memory, the story is nicely constructed to fit into Prince's psychological profile. An illicit act in an inappropriate place, above all an illicit act of *looking*; an older woman, but not a conventional 'older woman' and certainly not a mother figure; precocious desire met with an odd mix of adult denial, gentle humiliation, and permissiveness.

Light, costume, glamour, sex – the only element missing from the picture/memory is the one in which Prince was seemingly fated to spend the rest of his life. What music was John Nelson playing? Was it his father's performance rather than that conveniently archetypal dancer's attentions that turned Prince on? However ambivalent he felt about Nelson, the boy seems to have related to his father's performing and went to extraordinary lengths to surpass it.

There's sometimes confirmation in omission or denial. The one thing the movie version takes away from John Nelson is performance. *Purple Rain* is no more than semi-autobiographical, if it is even that, but it scatters important clues. Prince is cast as 'The Kid', a sulky, selfish wannabe who turns the basement of a shabby frame house into a softly lit laboratory of music and seduction. Upstairs, his parents fight and make up, fight and make up, and it isn't clear which disturbs The Kid more or whose attention he really covets. When he intervenes on his mother's behalf, he is slapped down. She is light-skinned (certainly light-skinned enough to be Italian, and actually played by a Greek actress) but passive and curiously anonymous. We last see her sitting wretchedly in the street with her back turned, perhaps to hide her bruises but also to suggest that she matters less to this story than the brooding figure of the man who beats her.

By contrast, the camera lingers on Francis L., a powerful, handsome man, caught between utter stillness and explosive violence, elegantly dressed for a world he seems disinclined to enter. The Kid's father is a frustrated and self-destructive artist, shut away in his own basement, playing exquisite piano in the darkness. The boy tracks him down there, roaring 'Motherfucker' through the empty house like some disco Hamlet. His fury abates as he listens to Francis play, but underneath the tenderness of the moment – for all its raunch, the movie's only convincing love scene – there is an act of denial. When The Kid asks if he writes down his songs, Francis puts a forefinger to his head: they're locked away there. It's a highly ambiguous gesture in the circumstances. A little later, Francis puts a gun to that same temple and shoots himself. In the aftermath, The Kid/Prince finds a locked trunk of unperformed compositions in the cellar, all of them signed Francis L. We see him take his father's place, creatively if not Oedipally. The most important object in the movie isn't the growling purple motorbike or the equally phallic guitar bought for him by Apollonia, the girl who sets free his oddly passive libido and then becomes a rival performer. The most important object in the film is Francis L.'s piano, its clinching frame another turned-back shot, this time of the son going about his father's business.

When the success of *Purple Rain* allowed Prince to move into a brand-new custom-built mansion, John was given the old purple house down from Paisley Park and a similarly coloured BMW; in return he gave Prince the white Thunderbird mentioned in 1988's 'Alphabet St'. John continued to show up in the star's entourage, with ever younger girlfriends. He was there for the ceremonial unveiling of the completed *Around the World in a Day* (1985), on which John L. Nelson has two co-writing credits. The father–son partnership continued on *Parade* with 'Christopher Tracy's Parade' and 'Under the Cherry Moon', and the rapprochement seemed firmly cemented by the time of the *Batman* soundtrack, made in 1989, which has one track, 'Scandalous', credited to Prince and Nelson Sr. Inevitably, though, like almost every Prince associate, John believed that other songs were at least partly his work and the relationship foundered. John wasn't present on Valentine's Day 1996 when his son married Mayte.

For a time, Prince had seemed keen to foster his father's career. There were other motives behind the call, but a decade earlier, Prince had picked up the phone to a former manager and sometime collaborator and asked him to listen to John Nelson's tapes and consider producing an album. Chris Moon was the mildly eccentric Englishman and adoptive Minneapolitan who wrote the original lyric to what became the title song of Prince's first album *For You*, or at least so he claimed. He and Prince parted company amicably enough – though there were copyright wrangles later – and it was Owen Husney who brokered the soon to be controversial contract with Warner Brothers. Whether Prince retained an affection for Moon, nursed a grudge or a sense of guilt depends on how you read the signs scattered in the work (the 'Christopher' pseudonym and the money obsession of *Under the Cherry Moon*). It is telling that Chris Moon should have been his first thought as the man to kickstart John Nelson's stalled career.

How much in turn Nelson had helped his son with his developing passion for music isn't known, presumably not much. The marriage foundered before Prince was in fourth grade. Thereafter, Prince was pretty much brought up by family friend Bernadette Anderson. Contact with his father was, for the time being, intermittent.

Interestingly, when Prince spoke to the BBC in 1981, he traced his interest in sexual themes to reading his mother's 'dirty books'. It's tempting to think that the stash of porn was really his father's, but it seems Mattie's idea of sex education was to give her son *Playboy* magazines to read. It hardly matters, because Prince quickly tired of other people's fantasies and started to write down his own.

Purple Rain offers only teasing glimpses of how things might have been or might have seemed to an imaginative boy. There is no complicating sibling in the movie, but two years after Prince was born John Nelson and Mattie Shaw had one other child, a girl christened Tyka (Tika Evene) who pops up in the release sheets for 1988 with an album for Chrysalis and then disappears again. John and Mattie drifted apart and were divorced in 1966, when Prince was nine. More unusual was their son's behaviour. Rather than split his loyalties, or plump for life with one parent rather than the other, Prince turned his back on both. Having left his mother and stepfather to live with John Nelson for a time, at thirteen he was ostensibly alone and self-sufficient. One persistent story suggests that he lived rough. This is a familiar element of myth, comparable to Bob Dylan's hobo days and Kurt Cobain's sojourn under the Aberdeen bridge. In reality Prince was being looked after by a family friend, a South Side neighbour and fellow Seventh Day Adventist called Bernadette Anderson, whose son Andre – later Andre Cymone – was a mainstay of the Grand Central band and Prince's most stimulating early musical associate.

The exact circumstances are, as usual, not entirely clear. Bernadette Anderson remembers that Prince had regular fall-outs with his dad, but that things came to a head when a girl, perhaps the first of many infatuated soul-girls, followed him home after a rehearsal night. According to Bernadette, his father threw the boy out of the house and he came to her. By the time this is supposed to have happened John Nelson had moved out and Mattie was living with a guy called Hayward Baker. He has an important role in the development of Prince the musician, because it seems he took the boy to see a James Brown concert and even put the ten-year-old up on stage to dance with the star, until a security man dragged him off. (According to Brown himself, Prince repeated the experience more officially in 1984, when he and Michael Jackson played guest spots, the three Hardest Working Men in Showbusiness together on the same stage.) However warmly he might have remembered that childhood epiphany, Prince was suspicious of his mother's new partner, and some former associates suggest that it was Baker and not John Nelson who beat him.

Prince continued to spend time with John. If the two were crashing in what was effectively a bachelor pad, there may well have been tensions if the son brought a girl home; or it may be that Baker was uneasy about a growing boy sharing the house on Fifth Avenue South and it was he who precipitated the final leave-taking. Whatever the case, it seems that Nelson gave his blessing to the new arrangement. As well he might have, since Bernadette Anderson was no ordinary woman, a tough, generous soul with a strong record in community activism. She is explictly thanked on the 1992 ♀ album: 'Bernadette the lady – she told me / Whatever U do, son, a little discipline is what you need.' (The track is the strange, autobiographical 'The Sacrifice of Victor', in which Prince adopts a new identity.)

Prince is not unusual in having, as well as a full sister, an array of step- and half-siblings. John Nelson had three children by his previous marriage – including Lorna Nelson, who claimed, unsuccessfully, to have written 'U Got the Look' – but the household also included Vivienne Nelson's child from a previous relationship; Prince's childhood companion Duane was later a Paisley Park employee, before falling foul of the law. Is he the brother 'handsome and tall' who's paid back in one of those vicious sexual thrusts in 'Lady Cab Driver'? Prince was also close to Mattie and Hayward's son Omar. Casual adoptions are not unusual and children are often raised by grandparents, aunts (Prince briefly attempted to move in with his aunt Olivia) and non-family members. It was generous if not heroic of Mrs Anderson to offer a home to yet another troubled adolescent. Selective versions of his time there provided media profilers with the first clues to what made Prince tick. In a crowded house, lines have to be drawn. The published legend deemed that at least one of them should be literal. Did Prince or Andre really run a strip of tape down the centre of their tiny bedroom? Real or invented, it separated Prince's fussy order from Andre's adolescent clutter and separated Prince from his immediate surroundings, an early token of what is either remoteness or a sign of intense powers of concentration. Bernadette later moved him into the basement, where he could order his life more comfortably.

More than any comparable artist, Prince has been a victim of the pop psychologists. Once you hear the work and see the performing self as consolation for a stolen childhood and overcompensation for small stature, Prince is reduced to his own fantastical creation. When at the age of twenty he released a record written, performed and produced entirely by himself, the media gratefully seized on an image of Prince as a precocious loner and equally gratefully accepted every perverse tidbit he threw their way. What makes *For You* (1978) an epoch in American popular music can't be explained by back-of-envelope psychology. To see Prince as a grubby child excitedly waving the treasure he's found is to be distracted by the glister. What is interesting about Prince is the dust rather than the gold. To understand him, one needs to understand the industry he helped to transform, and to understand Minneapolis.

3

In 1985 *Minneapolis Genius – The Historic 1977 Recordings* appeared on the Hot Pink label. This is the kind of tribute LP normally only accorded dead artists like Miles Davis, whose studio sweepings are now boxed and sold at platinum card prices. The music on it was in similar sketchy form, mostly shapeless instrumentals that cried out for a strong-handed producer, though one of them, 'If You Feel Like Dancing', later became a club favourite. The material was attributed to a band called 94 East, but the styling of the cover – purplish, with a white dove holding a rose in its bill – coupled with the Minneapolis provenance, was intended to leave potential purchasers in no doubt that this was a Prince product. A couple of years later, the notorious *Black Album* (1987, released 1994) would become the decade's most celebrated bootleg, but *Minneapolis Genius* has a prior place in the story.

There was no risk of ambiguity or confusion in the title. In 1985, there was only one genius in the Twin Cities and that was Prince. Back in 1977, when those tracks were cut, a television series that had strongly conditioned America's view of Minneapolis was just coming off the air, though only to enter the strange purgatory of the network repeat cycle. *The Mary Tyler Moore Show* was actually shot in California with a feisty Brooklyn girl as its protagonist, but Mary's lopsided grin and rueful stoicism in the face of eternal human stupidity spoke volumes about her Minneapolis home and workplace. Those Americans with a more political perspective might have remembered that Minnesota was the heartland of liberal Democrat hopeful Eugene McCarthy, who managed to survive 1968 unassassinated and sweetly irrelevant.

Almost everyone who lived there before the Prince revolution reflects a similar ambivalence. In the 1970s Minneapolis was a safe town and a dull town. An enviable record in civil rights and racial coexistence does not make a place funky. To that extent, Minneapolis was both the right and the wrong place for Prince to grow up: wrong in the sense that it lacked the deep roots in black music that could be taken for granted elsewhere, such as Detroit and Chicago; right in that it allowed him to develop at his own pace and on his own terms. In return, Prince created the brand new something that was called the Minneapolis sound. He also did what local boys made good often do and bequeathed the town a monument to his own success (or in Prince's case his own hyperactive self-determination), a version of Camelot and a more grown-up version of Michael Jackson's playpen Neverland. The Paisley Park studio complex sits about half an hour's ride outside

Minneapolis, alongside Highway 5, at 7801 Audubon Road in Chanhassen. It's now a bigger draw than the city's celebrated Museum of Questionable Medical Devices.

The extent to which Prince invented the Minneapolis scene has been endlessly debated. The mythological version likes to paint him as a younger, yet more potent version of a Fisher King, bringing energy and (purple) rain to a musically arid and sexless place. The more sober version points to a quiet infrastructure of studios, joints and rehearsal rooms, the world in which John Nelson worked away quietly. As so often in American stories, the mythological version wins out.

* * *

Remarkably, given where it sits on the North American continent, Minnesota is washed by the Mississippi. The great river is integral to black America and black American music. In slave narratives and sociological treatises, in the testimony of educated freedmen and in musical histories, the journey north is portrayed as a mystical portage up from bondage and towards liberation, a salmon ladder in terms of cultural evolution. It was, you'll still read it argued, the journey against the flow of the Mississippi that helped turn inchoate field hollers and marching tunes into Chicago blues and New York bebop, ultimately Detroit and Philly soul as well. If those cities far away from the headwaters felt its influence, why not Minneapolis?

In 1963, a year of acutely sharpened ethnic awareness in America and Prince's first year at grade school, the collective population of Minneapolis and St Paul was still well shy of two million. That figure included only about 50,000 African-Americans, mostly clustered up on the North Side, which made Minneapolis just 3 per cent black. Mattie Shaw was an exception. As black southerners moved north in search of economic opportunity, Minnesota stood aside from the demographic mainstream, as it had been since it became a territory (not yet a state) in 1849; in that year, just forty free persons of colour lived there. Between 1860 and 1870, deeply troubled years in American history, the censused black population rose from 259 to 759, largely as a result of freed slaves travelling north with Minnesotan soldiers. In the early years of the twentieth century, the black population of the state experienced a significant drop.

At a casual glance, the city seems to fit the usual urban American sociological stereotype of rich-white-quarter abutting poor-black-quarter. According to her recollection, in 1967 Prince and his sister Tyka were part of a 'bussing' experiment to desegregate Minneapolis schools. There is also a reference to this on 'The Sacrifice of Victor' from the ♀ album (1992). This was the direct result of a 1954 decision in the case of Brown vs the Board of Education in Topeka, Kansas, in which Supreme Court Justice Warren ruled that segregation of schools violated the Fourteenth Amendment to the Constitution and that the principle of 'separate but equal' was unconstitutional. The idea was to prevent the insidious ghettoisation of the inner cities by moving black schoolchildren into basically white catchments, and vice versa. Twenty years later, Milliken vs Bradley's revelation that there were deep flaws in that ruling were pounced on by the Reagan administration as it took a cost-cutting scythe to social services. The picture since has been one of steady resegregation, though slower, significantly enough, in the Twin Cities than elsewhere.

This is consistent with the area's long history of political liberalism. A decade after Milliken vs Bradley, Minnesota stood alone in its opposition to Reagan's presidential candidacy, pulling the switch for another forgotten man of American politics, Democrat Walter Mondale. In his study *The Negro in Minnesota* (1961) Earl Spangler points out that Minnesota was the first state to grant full suffrage to blacks under the terms of the Fifteenth Amendment. A similar picture emerges in June Drenning Holmquist's 1981 *They Chose Minnesota*, a survey of the state's ethnic groups, and in David Vassar Taylor's *Blacks in Minnesota* (1976) and his more recent *African-Americans in Minnesota* (2002) (Minnesota Historical Society/Press). There were notorious lynchings near Duluth in 1920, sparked as such episodes often were by alleged 'gross insult' to a white woman, but the obsessiveness with which these incidents are reasoned away as pathological aberrations in Minnesotan histories suggests that such acts of crude violence were by no means the norm. Here was a state with a markedly good record in interracial relations, if not quite a colour-blind paradise.

Five years after Prince and Tyka graduated from John Hay Elementary and started taking the bus a few blocks downtown to Bryant Junior High School, riots flared in Minneapolis as they did almost everywhere in urban America. Several businesses were burned and the police department, reckoned to be the most holstered and restrained in North America, went out and cracked heads. If raw statistics and the chaos theory of dissent mean anything, the violence in Minneapolis in 1968 wasn't a direct reaction to adverse social conditions. Clearly it was more than a television-fuelled carnival of destruction given a political and sociological rationale after the fact, but it was certainly not the ideologically driven ghettos-on-fire picture that had emerged that year across the continent. However few in number, blacks in Minneapolis enjoyed an easier coexistence with the white majority than they could have expected almost anywhere else. They lacked the critical mass to be defined as a major problem *or* to sustain a completely autonomous cultural development. And yet, in his song 'The Sacrifice of Victor', Prince refers explicitly to the riots as his moment of politicisation.

Compared to the average African-American teenager growing up in the larger cities of the north, Prince's musical heritage was disproportionately white. If it seems self-evident that his main influences as a performer were Sly Stone, Rick James and Jimi Hendrix, it's arguable that what he learned from each of them (and from Rick James at closer quarters when he opened for him on tour in 1979) was more about presentation than about music. The fact remains that much of the music Prince and his Minneapolis contemporaries listened to as teenagers was white pop and heavy rock. In February 1981, as *Dirty Mind* was taking off, Prince built on his nascent White Negro hipster-hoodlum persona by telling *Rolling Stone* that he'd grown up on an ethnic borderline. 'I had a bunch of white friends and a bunch of black friends. I never grew up in one particular culture.' It may have contributed to the mythology, but this part of it at least was true. It's worth remembering that Jimi Hendrix, born in Seattle long before Seattle was a real music town, made his name with English musicians and a pale Geordie manager, the late Chas Chandler.

The Twin Cities bequeathed Prince an unusual perspective on American popular music. Minneapolis is what is known in the business as a vanilla market. British observers of the American scene are still perturbed by how sharply and how overtly the music industry is segregated. At one time 'race records' were cut exclusively for a black market but even in the 1970s and 1980s, there were separate charts for rock and r'n'b, which despite an enthusiastic take-up of black music by white teenagers was still tantamount to segregating audiences. Radio airplay was crucial and radio stations were more than ever in the grip of advertisers armed with demographic models and spreadsheets. As Dave Hill put it in *Prince: A Pop Life*, 'Specific audiences were identified and catered to, in line with the dictates of commercials. And that "specialisation" effectively meant the resegregation of radio along racial lines that were no less rigid for justifying their informal apartheid with free-enterprise logic.'

In line with that relentless equation, Minneapolis had no infrastructure of black music stations. KMOJ had a virtual monopoly and thus a fairly safe, chart-driven playlist. For a time, KUXL offered smooth soul, classic Motown and some lite jazz to the small better-off black community on the South Side. All of which meant that even African-American youngsters of Prince's age were drawn to a diet of white progressive rock on KQRS. His early band Grand Central, which some remember, probably wrongly, as Grand Central Station, was around too soon to have been named after Larry Graham's mid-1970s funk unit Graham Central Station, though that might explain the confusion. (Graham later became a friend and something of a spiritual mentor, leading to the revelation in the late 1990s that Prince had followed his example and joined the Jehovah's Witnesses.) The band's later name-change to Champagne may well have been precipitated by optimistic recognition of a possible market clash, though it actually took place when Prince went to Central High, presumably so that it *wouldn't* sound like a school band. The original name – or rather the second name since the group briefly went out as Phoenix – may also have been a nod to white bicep rockers Grand Funk Railroad, later known by the fans' preferred short form

Grand Funk. Theirs was the kind of heavy, anthemic rock that Prince and his friends dabbled in, and who knows, the later addiction for performing half-naked and glossed with oil might just be a screen memory of Grand Funk guitarist Mark Farmer stripped to the waist and sweating his way through a falsetto 'Mean Mistreater'. Skinny kid looks at Charles Atlas advertisement and dreams.

For Prince's contemporaries, Grand Funk, Iron Butterfly and the James Gang, British acts like Led Zeppelin, Deep Purple and all the others that followed in the wake of the 'invasion' spearheaded by The Beatles and Herman's Hermits were every bit as immediately compelling as r'n'b. These were the groups that played uptown and these were the groups that got the local airplay. In 1978 when Prince released his first album the best known Minneapolis band were punk thunderers Hüsker Dü; a couple of years later, you might mention The Replacements as well. Though punk as such didn't make much impact on him, white rock and pop were to influence Prince's music from the beginning.

It's wrong to suggest that Minneapolis had no musical infrastructure, just that it was very different to those of Chicago or Philadelphia. The town's most important contribution to popular music was the retail system established by Amos Hellicher's distribution label Soma. By the late 1960s, though, it was living up to its name. People were being put to sleep by smooth, close-harmony romance and looking for a more resonant style of pop. There was also a thriving club scene in the Twin Cities, particularly in the knot of clubs and restaurants round Seven Corners, where John and Mattie Nelson played.

Records, gigs and radio are all influential, but what sparks many a career is a strong local role model, someone from the same background who makes good. Apart from his father, there was no one of a slightly older generation to emulate. Pianist Bobby Lyle is probably best known as MD to soul diva Anita Baker in the mid-1980s and from the smooth jazz of *Pianomagic* and 2004's *Straight and Smooth*. Lyle grew up in Minneapolis, and was known to John Nelson. His early records seem to have been released only in Japan and by the mid-1970s he was drifting away from jazz, and from the Twin Cities. In 1976, though, Lyle was working with Sly & the Family Stone and Prince would certainly have been aware of that.

While Prince's ferocious self-determination clearly didn't develop in a vacuum, there was no black Minneapolitan he could point to and say: I want to be him. The only internationally famous Minnesotan was Bob Dylan, who was born in Duluth and grew up in grimy Hibbing, where black skin probably meant you worked in the iron mill and washed off at the end of the day. There were bands around who proved it was possible to make a go of a musical career, even on a relatively unstructured scene like that of North Side Minneapolis and, given the scale of the place, it's inevitable that their histories intersect with Prince's. Flyte Tyme was perhaps the most successful of the basement groups, with a membership that included Terry Lewis,

Jellybean Johnson and later Jimmy Jam. It also featured a small horn section, which would not have endeared it to Prince, who was initially wary of horns. There was also another North Side band The Family (not to be confused with English rockers Family), for whom Prince later wrote 'Nothing Compares 2 U', best known from Sinéad O'Connor's cover version.

Jam and Lewis, who went on to be Janet Jackson's saviours, eventually co-opted the Flyte Tyme name for their production company, but by then the band had metamorphosed into Prince protégés The Time, who became an integral part of his scene-breaking tour packages, along with the shrewdly confected girl band Apollonia 6. Soul star Alexander O'Neal was proposed as vocalist for the new group, but declined; perhaps believing that Minneapolis wasn't big enough for Prince and himself; perhaps outraged at the money side of the deal; perhaps (as in one version) sacked for being 'too black', or possibly looking too much like Billy Eckstine for a funk-rock group. Five years older than the young Pretender, O'Neal's breakthrough nevertheless didn't come until 1985, by which time Prince was touring the multiple-platinum *Purple Rain*.

* * *

School friends remember him as Skipper (or Skippy) Nelson. The pet name came from his mother and might have been Mattie Shaw hitting back at her husband. Even if, as Jimmy

Jam remembers, most of it was platforms and the biggest 'fro anyone had ever seen, those who talk about Prince remember him as having *stature*, on and off the basketball court. Not everyone called him Skippy or Princess or Butcher Dog; he was also known as 'the Human Jukebox', the kid who knew every song going and who could reproduce them on a widening array of instruments. Some of his celebrated multi-instrumentalism and composer credits are on the material released on *Minneapolis Genius*, but there Prince is very much a group player. The 94 East material, originally intended for Polydor before that deal fell through, overlaps with the first work on what became *For You*.

His musical career seems to have begun at home, picking out tunes on John Nelson's piano. The first tune he learned to play is supposed to have been the television *Batman* theme, coincidentally given his later involvement with the Tim Burton movie. It's said that he wrote his first song at the age of seven, and it may well be that that first manuscript (possibly known as 'Funkmachine') is lying in the vaults at Paisley Park even now. Interestingly, no one who knew him in his early teens remembers him as a prodigy. Prince's 'genius' is more likely to have resulted from sheer hard work rather than some kind of Mozartian gift. There's a possible parallel here with Andy Warhol, the 'Picasso out of Pittsburgh', whose apparently enervated and will-less approach to work disguised a ruggedly industrial and intensely hard-working background; no coincidence that this son of a manufacturing town should call his studio 'the Factory'. It's significant, too, that one of the most important aspects of Prince's musical education was a business class. It was run at Central High by an easygoing former session player called Jim Davidson who taught students how to make and present demo tapes, as well as copyright, contract and other legal issues. Andre Anderson and Terry Lewis both took the class, but it was Prince who took the lessons most to heart. One wonders how often in later years he tried to apply Davidson's uncomplicated principles to his dealings with Warners, sacked band members and copyright claimants.

There was scarcely a moment in his teens when Prince was not making music, either alone or with the friends who formed his first band. Grand Central went through a number of personnel, including Prince's cousin Charles Smith, who seems to have been a respectable drummer. (He also introduced Prince to keyboard player Gayle Chapman.) He was probably better than his replacement Morris Day, who along with Andre Anderson and Prince formed the nucleus of the active band. There may have been an extra-musical reason for Day's recruitment, since his attic offered an alternative rehearsal venue to Prince's basement at the Anderson house. When they were working from home Andre's sister Linda sometimes played keyboards.

Until Prince was sidetracked – or monorailed – into making solo demos with Chris Moon, Grand Central and Champagne were the focus of his musical life. Recollections vary as to what they sounded like. One has to be wary of self-interest in the suggestion of band members that the roots of Prince's black music revolution lay in those chaperoned gigs in downtown bars, where the age limit was a rock-solid twenty-one. Most reliable witnesses remember a mix of lightly funked-up rock and jazz. Champagne was a faintly ironic banner for the abstemious and in those days not even studiedly frivolous Prince. No underage drinking for him, in fact nothing that got in the way of making music.

If his father was the key early influence, it was a cousin by marriage who helped steer him and Grand Central along a more professional route. Linster Willie – always known as Pepe – left New York for Minneapolis after marrying Shauntel Manderville, who was the daughter of Mattie Nelson's twin sister. Pepe had worked in and around the music business for some years, as a gofer for his uncle's band Little Anthony and the Imperials and as a freelance songwriter. He knew Prince and talked to him about music, but it seems that it was Morris Day's mother who suggested that he take Grand Central in hand. The first priority, as far as Willie was concerned, was to put the publishing situation on a proper footing, suggesting to Prince that he write to Broadcast Music Incorporated – the powerful BMI – and make sure that all songs were securely copyrighted. This was one area where Jim Davidson's Business of Music lessons seem not to have taken, and later it was to be the source of much disagreement.

Like just about every association in Prince's early life, this one ended acrimoniously, but for a time the cousins worked together effectively enough. Pepe helped streamline Prince's songs, which demonstrated more creative ambition than structure or market awareness; in 1977, the year before his debut record, Prince was playing on Pepe's own demos. They attracted some interest from Polydor, who were later set to release 94 East before that deal collapsed. Some of their overlapping work appears on *Minneapolis Genius* and Pepe Willie is the composer of the briefly successful 'If You Feel Like Dancing'. Given how his own career stalled apart from that one minor hit, it's not surprising that Pepe would lay claim to much of that material. Its real authors, though, were Andre and Pepe's talented cousin.

Prince had begun to spread his wings, both creatively and geographically. He found being a band member constraining, particularly when he didn't share their enthusiasm for white rum and beer. Andre – who later changed his second name to Cymone – dined out for a time on stories of adolescent exploits with Prince, but these read like a curious backward projection of the priapic star of *Purple Rain* and *Parade* onto the shy, almost puritanical kid. Prince's later affiliation to the Jehovah's Witnesses wasn't so much an aberration as a return to his church roots. Alcohol and drugs have never played a significant role in the Prince entourage.

Pepe Willie had contacts in New York. He had contacts all over the place. One of the local ones was keyboard player Gayle Chapman. Another resident of the white St Louis Park suburb that raised the Rivkins, she was to play an important but largely unrecognised role in the early Prince story, bringing not just musical skills but a strong Christian sensibility that seems to have reinforced Prince's notion that live performance had a sacred dimension. Pepe Willie knew her because they'd collaborated on songs. His more immediate value to Prince, though, was his knowledge of the New York studio scene. However important the Cookhouse and Studio 80 had been (and would continue to be, as witness the joint David Rivkin/Studio 80 thanks on *For You*), Prince's ambition needed more sophisticated facilities. Some of the instrumental material on *Minneapolis Genius* was taped in New York, from where Prince kept close and sometimes anxious contact with the man he'd asked to be his manager. It is to Chris Moon's eternal credit that he realised early that it would take someone with considerably heavier clout to manage 'the new Stevie Wonder'.

4

In 2004, Prince released an album called *Musicology*. Like the first two albums, it is neither bad nor great, and for much of its length merely competent. No one expected the forty-six-year-old to make another *Sign 'O' The Times*, or even a *Dirty Mind*, but after a run of indifferently received albums another disappointment would have rated as a technical knock-out. In the event, it wasn't so much treated as a win on points as a sign of recovery, the work of a man who'd come back from a very bad place, calm and rebalanced, less paranoid and vituperative. Prince was Prince again, no longer The Artist Currently Known As Wanker, 'Squiggle' or 'SLAVE'. In the first showcases, he spoke warmly in that unexpected baritone about loyalty to the fans who'd stuck with him, and he delivered an album full of gentle seduction (more Marvin Gaye than Rick James), jazzy soul and power pop.

The fans attributed much of its success to a set of words that appeared over several of the tracks. They were a reminder of where Prince had begun in 1978. The major credit line on *For You* reads 'Produced, Arranged, Composed and Performed by Prince'. Lest there be any ambiguity, the publisher details run 'All selections by Ecnirp Music Inc'. In *Prince: A Pop Life*, Dave Hill quotes the album's executive producer Tommy Vicari, somewhere between admiration and exasperation, asking Prince 'Why don't you press the record and take the picture as well?' No sooner said than ... 'Dust Cover Design by Prince'.

The actual photography on *For You* is by Joe Giannetti. It catches the producer/arranger/composer/performer/dust-cover designer in blurry soft focus, his towering Afro backlit, the look guarded rather than lustful or defiant. But for a shadow of moustache, it might almost be the young, pre-surgery Michael Jackson. It is a low-key image and it fits the product, because *For You* is certainly not the epoch sometimes claimed; like its distant successor *Musicology*, it now seems fussily competent rather than organically brilliant, interesting as a first exposure to Prince's distinctive coalition of funk, tv jazz and heavy rock, interesting above all for the circumstances in which it was made.

* * *

Central to the Prince mythology is that he was the first black musician to cut free of corporate interference and insist on control of every creative dimension of the music. Even if the latter part is true as read, he certainly wasn't the first. eBay browsers occasionally turn up albums by the Jimmy

Castor Bunch, in fact Jimmy Castor himself, as the silhouette-only images of the other band members might have given away. Jimmy played just about everything you heard. Somewhat up the creative scale was Stevie Wonder, who turned twenty-one in 1971, came of legal age and, benefiting from earlier in-fighting with the label by the self-driven Marvin Gaye, made what was effectively a shotgun contract with Motown which allowed him to write, produce and perform his own work.

By then, though, Stevie Wonder was a veteran, having been spotted by Berry Gordy at the age of ten, and with an enormous amount of second-hand studio knowledge and market awareness. Even so, Wonder's independence shouldn't be exaggerated. His greatest albums are the fruit of collaboration, specifically with synthesizer wizards Malcolm Cecil and Robert Margouleff of The Original New Timbral Orchestra, better known to record buyers of a certain age as Tonto's Expanding Headband. When Stevie split with them later, convinced he'd mastered their skills for himself, his work went into sharp decline. By the same token, Prince's celebrated independence on *For You* and after needs to be examined more closely.

The only exception to Prince's sole credit on *For You* and the reason there's a little asterisk beside 'Composed' is that the lyrics to the album's first single 'Soft and Wet' are attributed to 'Prince and C. Moon'. He's the same C. Moon who's thanked along with God, Mum and Dad, Bernadette Anderson and a slew of Minneapolis friends and bandmates.

He's also the same Christopher Moon who turned up in the office of the Minneapolis businessman Owen Husney announcing he'd found the next Stevie Wonder.

Both white men – Moon is English by birth and Husney Jewish – play a central part in the Prince story. Husney's advertising background allowed him to lay siege to the major labels in the most blatant way. His schtick was a good one. Here was a black kid from Minneapolis – virgin territory as far as New York and San Francisco executives were concerned – who played all the instruments and sang all the voices on Moon's demo tape. If his first reaction was surprise and delight – and Husney was an amateur musician with a bit of band experience – then surely there was someone out there who'd share that response and clinch it with a signature?

Moon's role is more ambiguous. Though he's only listed as co-lyricist on one track, he later claimed part-authorship of several more – including 'Baby' and 'My Love is Forever' on *For You* – and money changed hands nearly a decade later to settle the matter. Moon was one of the few people in Minneapolis who ran a professional sound studio and it was there, at Moon Sound in the south of the city, that he came into contact with Champagne and with Prince Nelson. Ironically, Moon may have been the catalyst for Prince's firing from the group, ostensibly for spending too much time on his solo projects. Either way, the tall Englishman and Skippy Nelson made an inseparable pair for a time; an unlikely pair, too, tall and short, white and black, some distance apart in age, but both sporting tall Afros and both obsessed with music.

What exact contribution Moon made to Prince's nascent career is now lost in the divide that opened up between them, and sealed away by the lawyers. However, it seems clear that Prince maintained an ambivalent attitude to his old collaborator, part-gratitude, part-guilt, part-anger. Dave Hill points to the curious moment in the film of *Under the Cherry Moon* when Prince – or rather the success-hungry 'Christopher' – sits up in bed looking at a piece of paper that shows a large 'C' and a waning moon. Release of the film and album coincided with Moon's legal settlement with Prince and Controversy Music, so the reference is unlikely to be random.

From here on in the Prince story, the most familiar stock character is the old friend and associate who feels he made a significant contribution to the superstar's career, only to be snubbed and possibly stiffed out of money owed. Prince fell out spectacularly with his cousin Pepe Willie over the unauthorised (by him) release of the 94 East tapes on *Minneapolis Genius*, presumably forgetting that Willie didn't have a *Purple Rain* flying off the shelves at the time. Other claims are less secure, like Andre Anderson's that he had contributed in some substantial way to *For You*. No one else remembers him doing much, other than as a friend and supporter. Certainly there's no sign of Andre's popping bass among Prince's own Orr and synth bass patterns.

Significantly, Andre – one of the 'heaven-sent helpers'

on the eponymous second record – isn't thanked on the album credits, though his mother Bernadette Anderson is, just after God, Owen and Britt Husney, and just before the Nelsons – 'My Father and Mother'. After that comes Russ Thyret, the Warner Brothers vice-president who beat CBS and A&M to the punch, signed up Prince and ultimately agreed to let him self-produce. Quite how he was persuaded is the stuff of industry legend – it seems senior production staff were asked to 'drop by' the L.A. studio where Prince was demoing and pronounced him well up to the task – but it didn't stop Thyret insisting on putting someone in overall charge of the project. Tommy Vicari is listed as executive producer.

Husney's aim was to have made the first record in Minneapolis, home ground for Prince and unfamiliar turf for Warner Brothers high command. There's still a casual legend that *For You* was somehow put together in Prince's bedroom, a nonsense given its relatively high-tech resources and ambitious – if ultimately callow – production values. It's also at variance with the facts. The album was largely made at the Record Plant in Sausalito, California, with Vicari and Prince vying for engineering control. There was invaluable help, too, from David Rivkin of Sound 80 Studios in Minneapolis, where some of Prince's demos had been done. His role on the project has never been made specific, but in later years Rivkin remained a friend and associate of the increasingly solitary and paranoid Prince. His brother Bobby, known as Bobby Z, had been replacement drummer with the 94 East set-up and was to become part of Prince's touring band, sporting the least convincing moustache on the liner photograph of 1980's groundbreaking third album.

Dirty Mind came along symbolically on the cusp of a new decade and with a raw new sound that was to exert a root-and-branch influence on the r'n'b and rock of the 1980s. In 1978, even with a sympathetic team in place, Prince wasn't quite ready for the revolution.

* * *

For You isn't a shocking record, but it is a surprising one. The angular grind of later sets isn't yet in evidence and the mood is romantic rather than blatantly erotic. It begins with Prince *a capella*, singing the almost prayer-like title track, over a vast choir of subtly multi-tracked Princes. 'All of this and more is for you / With love sincerity and deepest care, / my life with you I share'. His falsetto establishes the album's vocal characteristic from the start, but it also instils a mood that combines many things that contribute to the Prince enigma: beautifully faked sincerity, a childlike combination of seriousness and play, desire expressed as gift rather than command. Dave Hill says of the brief track, little over a minute in duration, 'It is, at root, a display of devotion and personal sacrifice – a thoroughly Christian gesture.'

How many of its first listeners heard that opening benediction while looking at the other liner photograph? Multi-exposure is an obvious visual rhyme with Prince's multi-tracked studio style but the image is more than that. It shows Prince – or rather, three Princes – naked but for a large-bodied acoustic guitar, sitting cross-legged on a pile of quilts that seems to be floating in space. The light above him could be a nimbus or it could be the illuminated panel of a Wurlitzer jukebox. He looks less like the Holy Trinity than the avatars of some fierce and erotic young Hindu deity.

There is always a danger with an artist as self-conscious as Prince of reviewing the imagery rather than the music, but it's clear here more than anywhere in Prince's work that the visual context provides a strong clue as to how the record should be heard. In that regard, Hill's observation is very shrewd. There is something oddly sacrificial about *For You*, a very different mood to the erotic aggression of *Dirty Mind*. Even the adolescent sleaze of 'Soft and Wet' (which earned a ban on more sensitive radio stations) lacks absolute conviction. But then, it is a record made by a twenty-year-old, only technically still a teenager as the label and some of the press were anxious to convey.

It is quite patently a summing up of everything Prince knew to date, a record made with the kind of obsessive care that suggests he might have worried whether there really would be a follow-up, as the Warner contract provided, or whether he'd flop. Musically, it's no masterpiece, and for all Prince's attempts to clear his head of other sounds (even allegedly banning Stevie Wonder records from the studio speakers during breaks), it's still largely derivative. It's also said that Prince ran into his idols Sly Stone and Carlos

Santana during the making of the record, and slipped back into fan mode. Even so, *For You* does point the way forward and its structure is subtler than first appears. The longer side one is full of barely suppressed sexual desire. 'In Love' ripples with innuendo, while on the other side of 'Soft and Wet', the record's sparsest track 'Crazy You' is punctuated by hissing breaths that suggest jerking off rather than actual love-making; from a less prurient perspective, it's also a good early example of Prince's genius as a rhythm guitarist, slapping out chords on that big acoustic, and as a fine rhythm technician, using cymbals, chimes and water drums to give the track its oddly disembodied feel.

The dramatic turn of the original LP is lost on CD. Side one ended with a change of pace and mood. 'Just as Long as We're Together' is the album's longest track, edited for single release (b/w 'In Love'), and a change of pace from throbbing techno funk to soundtrack jazz. Turn the record over and what you have is one of the songs disputed with Chris Moon. 'Baby' is a tale of unwanted pregnancy, bordering on sentiment but sung with real drama and accompanied by a backing that for the first time shows the full range of Prince's instrumental mastery. It also shows how he managed to avoid a generic 'with horns' sound by reproducing horn parts on keyboards. The tech spec has Prince doing all the voices, acoustic and electric guitars, acoustic and Fender Rhodes piano, Orr bass, Mini-Moog, Oberheim 4-Voice, Arp Soloist, orchestra bells and drums. For the first time on the record, he doesn't sound like a kid loose in a music store, but more like the visionary musician he was to become.

The next two tracks, 'My Love is Forever' and 'So Blue' (which was the flipside to the first single), are a partial return to the mannered funk of 'In Love'. The final track is a surprise, or would have been to an r'n'b audience. 'I'm Yours' is thematically the musical bookend to 'For You'. It's no less of a studio confection, except that this time Prince attempts to replicate the live, guitar-dominated sound of AOR. It's the most explicit nod to the white acts that played such a part in his musical education. Heard cold and out of context, it might sound like a slice of bland poodle-rock, but it is subtler than that, the beginnings of a synthesis and a first gesture in the direction of musical biracism. It also provides the format for the guitar-orgasm of 'Purple Rain', a few years down the line.

* * *

It was the moment when Russ Thyret's gamble finally paid off. Released on April 7, 1978, *For You* represented only a modest return on Warner's investment, peaking at a below-the-radar 163 in the *Billboard* pop chart; doing better, but not spectacularly, in the black chart. It peaked there at twenty-one, but the fact that it stayed in the chart for nearly six months suggested that the r'n'b audience was slowly wakening to this weird-looking kid from a place no one had heard of, who apparently played all his own instruments.

Not until August 1979 did Prince score a number one single in the black chart, a feat he wasn't to repeat until the massive crossover success of 'When Doves Cry' five years later. 'I Wanna Be Your Lover' is the first genuine musical epoch in Prince's career, almost as original as 'Doves' in its blend of black funk and white pop, though not yet so boldly subversive in form. It has a bass-line, for a start, though interestingly its absence wouldn't rob the track of all its drama. The other components are equally familiar, vocals, guitar, synth, drums, but Prince was already experimenting with new ways of driving a song other than hanging it on the bass. One of them was to establish a tense, yearning dissonance in the very opening bars and then sustain it through the whole track. Guitar, synthesizer and drums do the bulk of the work; the bass is secondary and not so much structural as functional. What associates called his *'mubadib'* or *'blubalip'* style on the bass was not much more than a percussive slapping, doubtless influenced by Larry Graham's work with Sly Stone and similar to Bernard Edwards' with Chic, but far less subtle. It might be argued that of the twenty-six instruments Prince can play, the one he has mastered least confidently is the one that usually anchors black funk and soul. It can equally be argued that his musical vision was based on something rather different, an approach to harmonic tension and release that is almost physical, carried on the rhythm guitar (on which Prince is a – possibly *the* – unquestionable master) and which has less need for a strong bass.

It's a formula that comes more obviously from white pop, and notably from The Beatles. The final '*Yeah*' of 'She Loves You' is ambiguous in the way much of Prince's harmonic organisation is ambiguous, though its intent rarely is. So carefully conceived and crafted is 'I Wanna Be Your Lover' that only if you switch off the stereo and read the lyric instead – 'I ain't got no money / I ain't like those other guys you hang around' – is it possible to hear it as a conventionally romantic expression. No hearts and flowers; the song *embodies* lust and physical longing in every measure, which is why it became a dancefloor favourite that sold a million copies.

It was also chosen to preview and head off the sophomore album, which interestingly was self-titled, as if both Prince and Warner recognised that they had to start over and this time sell the star as much as the product. *Prince* (1979) built on a minor legend, probably better known within the industry than with the audience, still virtually unknown to live audiences outside the Twin Cities. Prince himself was in no doubt of his priorities. He told a reporter from the *Los Angeles Times* that he 'had put himself in a hole with that first record. I wanted to remedy that with the second album. I wanted a "hit" album.' It was a short-term ambition for an artist who explicitly didn't want the kind of fickle audience who only turned up to hear reruns of past hits, but for the moment that was the audience he had.

Prince also helped to establish his reputation as a songwriter for other people. Later years would see him contribute songs under a bizarre array of aliases, and for (mostly female) singers as diverse as Sinéad O'Connor, The Bangles and Sheena Easton, but also Kenny Rogers; another country icon, Dolly Parton, declined a similar offer, thus denying pop possibly one of the most bizarre creative partnerships imaginable. Chaka Khan had made her LP debut the same year as Prince, in 1978; then, just as *Purple Rain* signalled his apotheosis, she had a number three hit with what had been the penultimate track on *Prince*, a song originally written for jazz pianist and solo performer Patrice Rushen, with whom Prince was said to be in love.

One of the oldest tracks on the set, 'I Feel For You' cements the album's blatant emphasis on physical desire over romance: 'It's mainly a physical thing . . .', 'I'm physically attracted to you . . .' The tiny purple heart that dots the *i* of his name on the cover is just there for show. The harmonic tension of 'I Wanna . . .' flags up what the rest of the album then confirms: Prince wants to be your lover, in the most basic and unapologetic way. But not necessarily in an obvious or conventional way. What is striking about *Prince* is the way it plays with sexual roles and stereotypes. 'Sexy Dancer' has him lusting after some lap-and-pole girl: 'you got my body screamin' . . . you got me just-a-creamin' . . .', a playground rhyme that perfectly fits the adolescent thrust of the song. 'When We're Dancing Close and Slow' masquerades as a tender love ballad, but Prince isn't afraid to admit that even as they slowly rotate under the glitterball 'Sex-related fantasy is all that my mind can see', and he isn't bothered that his hard-on is becoming obvious: 'Can't you feel my love touching you?'

There's more to it, though. In 'Still Waiting', frustration tips over into self-loathing. Prince parodies a classic 1950s crooner with 'People say that I'm too young / Too young to fall in love'. He's sick and tired of being alone, feeling that life hasn't ended, it hasn't even begun. Where 'Baby' was a self-conscious injection of social seriousness on the first album, 'Still Waiting' injects a measure of emotional realism on the second, an element of Prince's songcraft and approach to album-building that's often overlooked. It also sounds remarkably like a country song, which makes the later Rogers/Parton connection seem less unexpected. He does something similar in emotional terms on the track that became the second – less successful – single. 'Why You Wanna Treat Me So Bad?' reads like the plaint of an older man, no longer able to satisfy his woman, put bluntly – 'You used to love it when I'd do you / You used to say it was the best you'd ever had' – but with genuine pathos.

This time round, he put his rock anthem in the middle of the set, rather than at the end. 'Bambi' is an astonishing song, not least because it's addressed to a lesbian – 'Bambi, it's better with a man' – but also because the lyric is so at odds with the roaring, guitar-laden instrumental track, the most full-on before 'Purple Rain'. What adds a certain piquancy to the track is that 'Bambi' is also thanked in the credits, suggesting Prince may have been venturesome in his private life as well as in the studio.

He was giving nothing away, however. A notorious television appearance on Dick Clark's *American Bandstand* had begun a reputation for extreme reticence. Clark got nothing but nods and shakes (anticipating the days when 'Prince' would turn up for interviews in a beekeeper's veil and relay monosyllabic answers via an intermediary), and a casually gestured '4' when Clark asked him how long he'd been playing. It was as uncomfortable a clash of styles and personalities as The Doors' encounter on *Ed Sullivan*, when Jim Morrison refused to change the 'higher' reference in 'Light My Fire'. Different versions exist. Some suggest Prince had decided in advance not to play ball; others suggest he was offended by a slighting comment about Minneapolis. Either way, he was no more prepared to talk about his music than he was to talk about his sexuality and beliefs.

Unless, of course, you accept that *Prince* 'Produced, Arranged, Composed* and Performed by Prince' is auto-biographical, albeit in the way that *Purple Rain* was to be autobiographical, which is to say selectively at best. What it is, certainly in comparison to the first album, is a beau-tifully confected pop artefact, not yet revolutionary in style, still very dependent on a grab-bag of musical influences, but emotionally inflected and satisfying as a whole. Marvin Gaye's fight with Motown had been over their insistence that a record album should consist of two hits and ten tracks of filler. *Prince* is no *What's Going On?*, not least because the second single limped no higher than number thirteen in the black chart and made no impact on pop sales, but it is a carefully conceived and executed work that deserves more attention than it gets.

The Prince that looks out from the cover this time is more vulnerable. Again naked but only seen quarter-length, fully lit and unguarded, his hair is arranged in a deliberately feminine style that chimes awkwardly with the moustache. A diamond stud sparkles in his right ear. The album's better known image has him naked and blurred with movement astride a winged white horse. If the one suggests a certain adolescent purity (and confusion), the other hints at a messianic complex. Neither of them hints at a dirty mind, and nothing on the album more than hints at what was going to come on *Dirty Mind*.

5

On *For You* and *Prince*, he came across as a horny choirboy, a more than averagely talented but otherwise in every way average black pop kid hovering on the uneasy cusp between teen romance, with its aura of awkward seriousness, and adult desire. A couple of years later, Michael Jackson would negotiate the same step in his own initially successful, later disastrous way. *Dirty Mind* (1980), though, was the one where Prince sang about fucking his sister and coming all over a bride's dress as she blows him on her way to the altar.

It's also the album where Prince started running with a gang. They're pictured on the inside sleeve, posed against a wall tagged with their graffiti names, looking like they might have been too smartly dressed for *The Warriors*. Prince is in his trenchcoat; Andre cops his look and moves as usual; Bobby Z is the token white boy who buys the liquor and diverts the cops; Dr Fink hides behind shades and a surgical mask and comes on less like a physician than a member of The Treatment; guitarist Dez Dickerson wears chef's check trousers under the requisite coat; Lisa Coleman, who'd come in as keyboard replacement for Gayle Chapman, is sweet but hard. That was the touring band. Chapman, blonde and beautiful, had moved on after Prince took to French-kissing her on stage during the live set's climactic 'I Wanna Be Your Lover'. A devout Christian as well as a formidable player, she found the contradictions in Prince's philosophy hard to accept, virtually guaranteeing she'd be sacked.

The irony of that group image was that of all Prince's records, *Dirty Mind* was the one he really did make on his own. Lisa adds a single-line vocal to 'Head', while Fink plays some synth on it and the title song, where he's listed as co-writer. Apart from that, it really was all produced, arranged, composed, et cetera, by Prince. He even fulfilled an ambition that had been thwarted at Burbank in 1978 of driving the desk as well as playing all the instruments. Engineer 'Jamie Starr' is just the first of many Princely pseudonyms. There was very little post-production tinkering. The album was released pretty much as demoed and in the order Prince dictated. Warner confirmed a reputation for liberal indulgence of exceptional talent by passing it on the nod – Russ Thyret and new president Larry Waronker (who'd run his eye over Prince during the *For You* sessions) were both supporters – and with only a minor edit to the original, apparently interminable version of 'Head'.

Significantly, the album was made back home in Minneapolis, or as he preferred to describe it on the album sleeve 'somewhere in Uptown'. This was a neat way of underlining the growing mystique of a solitary genius whose albums just appeared and who still wasn't a major live act, but 'Uptown' was also a mythical place. The name itself suggests Utopia, though it probably also had more local and personal associations. The cover portrays Prince as a version of Norman Mailer's hipster-hoodlum White Negro, which is very much the stylistic pitch of the music. Now drawing on punk aesthetics and New Wave philosophy, Prince passes himself off as a sociopathic pervert, living on a sexual, racial and sociological borderline. It's worth pointing out that in black idiom, 'punk' still carried its prison connotation of homosexuality. A less familiar image from the *Dirty Mind* session sees Prince all but naked in a shower cubicle, looking like a seedy rent boy. Significantly, there's a crucifix on the wall behind him. Almost the whole point of the inner sleeve photograph was that it *didn't* depict a band, or at least not a band responsible for the music you were about to hear, but a bunch of individuals secure in their polymorphous rejection of ordinary codes and conventions. The raucous party on the track 'Uptown' is a carnival of opposites and oddities.

It's ironic that at a time when Prince was decoupling himself from most of the familiar indices by which corporate labels judge marketability, Warner and the management team of Cavallo, Ruffalo and Fargnoli (mainly Steve Fargnoli) were trying to pitch him to two different audiences, black and white. It is as if they got the main point, saw its economic potential, but didn't quite get the subtler inflections, which

suggested that Prince was looking to a new constituency altogether. Something similar happened when Miles Davis
abandoned his bebop and cool past and started to play rock
and street funk, and found himself supporting the Steve
Miller Band. Prince would eventually find himself opening
for the Rolling Stones, disastrously; but that was in the future.
Warner were also aware that songs about incest and spunk
weren't going to attract a lot of commercial airplay. *Dirty
Mind* was going to depend on a different kind of visibility.

The cover photograph was taken by Minneapolis
commercial artist Allen Beaulieu. It shows Prince all but
naked under his trenchcoat, wearing nothing but tiny black
briefs and with a cowboy bandanna round his neck. The
back cover photograph reveals him in black stockings.
Beaulieu thought the image would be more arresting,
certainly more fleshly, in colour, but Prince shrewdly thought
different. The cover hasn't the scuzzy, headachey approxi-
mate focus of many punk albums of the time, but it is
visually unsettling, not least when you recognise that Prince
is posed against what look like abstract spirals and diamonds
but turn out to be bedsprings. As a declaration of intent
and as a way of detourning the usual presentation of sexy
black singers as boudoir Romeos, it couldn't be much rawer.

* * *

Such was Warner Brothers' commitment to their young and
potentially difficult rising star that there was never any

question of cancelling his contract or compromising his freedom of movement, even after the modest returns on his first two albums. However, the label was not convinced that Prince, or more fairly, Prince and his band, were ready to be launched as a major touring act. It isn't clear whether it was ever suggested that he be teamed with a more experienced group, either seasoned session men or recruits from existing units with a strong market profile. It's inconceivable that the idea never came up, and it's to Prince's eternal credit that he resisted it out of loyalty to his Minneapolis friends (the upside of his 'Napoleon syndrome').

The Warner hierarchy had come to the Twin Cities in January 1979, nine months after the release of *For You*, to watch the second of a three-show residency at the old Capri Theatre on Minneapolis's West Broadway. It was probably optimistic to think that a one-record act without a strong fan base even at home could fill the former cinema even on a benefit night, but it wasn't so much poor attendance as the chaotic nature of the gig that convinced the men in suits that Prince needed another record at least to establish a presence. They were, however, surprised, possibly shocked, by his stage presence, the absolute antithesis of the almost pathologically shy and reticent youngster they'd been dealing with through Husney and his brief replacement Don Taylor. Taylor came to Prince after working with Bob Marley, and left as quickly, convinced that the kid from Minneapolis was higher-maintenance than the reggae superstar.

In career terms, *Prince* was a less significant consolidation than the growing confidence of the touring band. Given that much of Prince's work wasn't radio-friendly, even before *Dirty Mind* ('Soft and Wet' had been too explicit for many stations), his reputation would build round the live act. A studiedly unpredictable approach to interviews didn't seem to be hurting Prince's visibility, either, but capriciousness, by definition, isn't a controllable strategy.

The Stones tour imbroglio in 1981 was an attempt, possibly misguided, to break Prince with a white rock audience. The final signifier on the *Dirty Mind* cover was a lapel button with a checkerboard background reading 'RUDE BOY'. It had been issued by the British 2-Tone label, who at the time were having chart success with multiracial bands like The Specials and The Selecter who played a blend of white pop, ska and reggae. Prince would certainly have heard songs like 'A Message to You, Rudy' on Minneapolis radio, but the 'rude boy' label, originally applied to Jamaican hoodlums, fitted the bill. In 1980, he was booked to tour with another, briefly successful crossover artist who'd co-opted a quasi-Rastafarian look and stance to his own blend of funk and rock.

Rick James also grew up away from the music mainstream, though Buffalo was near enough to New York for James to absorb some of its melting-pot eclecticism. James sported a version of dreadlocks in a stage act that resembled something of the cartoon character of George Clinton's P-Funk, though without its superb musicianship and subtle parodic layers. His presence on the scene is another indication that Prince didn't emerge entirely in a vacuum. James's Stone City Band, with its obvious reference to Sly's outfit, made an impact on Prince's later Revolution and New Power Generation line-ups, while Rick's clownishly lascivious manner chimed with his own.

There are various reasons for the rivalry which developed between them on their 1980 tour. They were perhaps too similar to be comfortable with one another. More important, Prince was unmistakably on the way up, young and full of energy, while the twenty-eight-year-old James had had his moment in the spotlight and was beginning to fade. Finally, and stereotypically, Prince stole his girl. At some point during the tour, Denise Matthews came over to Prince's bus and never left. A year or two further on, she had changed her name to Vanity and was fronting Vanity 6, one of his new stable of acts. The rolling stone from Minneapolis was gathering no moss, but he was picking up a caravan of followers.

* * *

If Prince was too black a year or two later for the Rolling Stones crowd (and there's no point dwelling on the irony of that) he was too white for the Rick James fans. Certainly too white for James himself who later accused his young rival – or 'little science fiction creep' – of turning his back on people of colour. The point was that in 1980 it was increasingly hard to tell where Prince's musical loyalties lay or where he sat in the market.

One of the new songs previewed on the tour was the now notorious 'Head'. It stands as a robust answer to James's carping. The beat is pure black funk, as is 'Do It All Night', on which Prince shows that he can do a bassline with the best of them. *Dirty Mind* kicks off with the title track, co-written with Matt Fink and significantly the most straightahead cut on the set. It establishes a certain mood, lewd, priapic, determinedly unsubtle, but as always Prince knows how to establish and then puncture listeners' expectations. Straight after it comes 'When You Were Mine', the kind of thing the Jackson Five might have been doing a few years earlier, a delightful piece of bubblegum soul that makes you think you're maybe not going to have to listen on cans after all. 'Do It All Night' and 'Gotta Broken Heart Again', the album's weakest cut, complete the first side and continue the game-playing.

Side two goes for the jugular. 'Uptown' celebrates Prince's new constituency, not yet Rainbow Children or even a Rainbow Coalition, but a kind of night-world in which all the cats are grey. The title might also be another of his unconscious, possibly guilty, associations, since Pepe Willie's house on Upton Avenue had been an important location when the group was rehearsing for the road. The song was to cause another slippage in Prince's worsening relations with another old friend and collaborator; Andre Cymone always claimed he'd had a hand in the writing. There is another, unsubstantiated story that the album's last cut, 'Partyup', was actually written by Morris Day, but that Prince took credit for it in exchange for a support slot for The Time on upcoming tours. If the story is true, it was an arrangement that rebounded badly on Prince when he took *Controversy* – and The Time – on the road in 1982.

Steered by Warner, Prince did a huge amount of publicity for *Dirty Mind*, much of it on the telephone, and used it to start building the mythology that would follow him in one distorted form or another for the rest of his career. At the time, almost everyone was asking what the girl on 'Uptown' asks him: is Prince gay? The remainder of side two of *Dirty Mind* – all 'real life stories', said the star – suggests that if he was sexually perverse, it was poly-morphously so. 'Head' is an epic, while 'Sister' gains its impact from being as brief as the singer's underwear. It is difficult to reconstruct now just how shocking and unex-pected these songs were on first release. Pop stars had always talked dirty. There was the mumbled smut of the Kingmen's classic 'Louie Louie' and Little Richard's exuberant innu-endo, but Prince brought something new and unnervingly direct. As ever, the shock value of the lyrics and their presumed autobiographical element usefully diverts the listener from the sheer artifice of the instrumental tracks, but with the passage of time it also helps refocus the listener on how shockingly new the instrumental components are. Despite that momentary concession to black funk bass, the key element again is the rhythm guitar. *Dirty Mind* is as harmonically subtle as it is verbally blatant. The real sucker punch is in the arrangements, though as yet 'Jamie Starr''s engineering skills aren't quite up to the composer's ambitions. Technically, it's still the work of a clever child, full of inchoate badness and shock for shock's sake.

* * *

That *Controversy*, which followed almost exactly a year later in 1981, represents a companion work is evident from the cover. The same studded trenchcoat and RUDE BOY button, but this time Prince is clad and in colour, looking like a cross between a riverboat gambler, charismatic frontier preacher and judge. No bedsprings behind him, either, but a splash of front pages from *The Controversy Daily*, the imaginary news sheet of Prince's imaginary 'Uptown' constituency. Some of the headlines smack of high-school mock-ups from a civics class: PRESIDENT SIGNS GUN CONTROL ACT, FREE FOOD STAMPS FOR GOOD SAMARITANS, ANNIE CHRISTIAN SENTENCED TO DIE! Some have an element of cut-up: PRESIDENT DECLARES UPTOWN NEW U.S. CAPITOL (sic), TOURIST INVASION OF UPTOWN FAILS, 89 BEHEADED! One simply reads: *JONI*. Of the others, three stand out: THE SECOND COMING, LOVE THY NEIGHBOR, DO YOU BELIEVE IN GOD.

At its worst, *Controversy* is preachy and judgemental. Strictly speaking, at its worst, it's very bad indeed. 'Jack U Off' is almost self-parody, while the short 'Ronnie, Talk to Russia' and the weird, robotic 'Annie Christian' fail as satire, and make for uncomfortable listening. Annie – an obvious reference to the Antichrist who gave her name to a Scottish indie band of the 1990s – is intended as a symbol for all that has gone wrong with an America defined by murder and assassination, a spirit of violent misrule whose perverse rationale and sole motivation is to make the tabloid headlines. There were those who dared to think Prince came closer to autobiography here than he strictly intended.

For all his references to public events, including the still recent shooting of John Lennon and the Atlanta child murders, he came no closer than before to coherent politics. The gesture was there, however. *Controversy* (a title also adopted for his publishing company) marked the end of Prince as guiltless fucker and the beginning of Prince the spokesman for a brand of sexual licence that is not so much libertarian as libertine, commingled inexplicably with religious redemption. Prince was no longer just a musician offering routine thanks to God, but a Musician with a Message. The difficulty was in telling what the message was: sex is good; sex is God; violence is bad, and thus the very Devil. Or perhaps the difficulty was just in telling who Prince now was: an avatar, a rebel who turned out to be a divinely appointed messenger; or maybe just part of the Spectacle.

If it was all intended as a sign that he was growing up as an artist (and that was hinted at in the opening track 'Controversy' itself, where he drops his trademark falsetto), all it proved was how much growing up he had to do. It's a curious and muddled album, partly redeemed by the title track's definitive blend of guitar and synthesizer with a new group vocal sound that anticipated the Sly Stone-influenced shared front line of '1999' almost two years later; redeemed, too, by such gems as 'Do Me, Baby' (nearly eight minutes of pure pop delight) and 'Private Joy', a title that by this point hardly needs decoding.

With Prince, a certain self-consciousness came as standard, but thus far nothing like the sulky pout of the cover picture or the petulant whinny of 'Controversy', which basically takes the media to task for their reaction to *Dirty Mind*, all that prurient copy about his race and sexuality. Nothing more hapless than a celebrity who courts publicity and then complains of it. If we were expected to take 'Prince' as a fictional character, the way 'Uptown' is an imaginary place, the blurring of documentary fact and PR mischief could have been better handled, the play-acting more securely staged in a fantasy world rather than a Minneapolis North Side suddenly invested by music hacks looking for the scuttlebutt on pop's most enigmatic new star. With *Controversy*, the Thurber question again comes into play: what do you want to be enigmatic *for*, Cynthia?

When, on 'Controversy', he recites the Lord's Prayer in the deadest, flattest voice imaginable, is he being blasphemous or is he so tired of the whole *schtick* – the murderous world of 'Annie Christian', the endless humping that follows in 'Do Me, Baby' – that rote religion is his only weary solace? If it goes any deeper than that, why put it first on the album, rather than as its destination, and why then immediately revert to the priapic thump of 'Sexuality'?

More questions than answers, then. In career terms, *Controversy* did no more than play into the media's hands and because the media's grasp on a collective cultural unconscious is always stronger than any individual's, even one who produces, arranges, composes, performs *and* drives the publicity, it saw Prince's self-created image take on an awkward momentum of its own; ever after, he struggled to control how the media and the music business saw him. In a curious way, though, the album was more damaging and less significant to his long-term reputation than the tour that promoted it.

* * *

Controversy was Prince's first major sortie as headliner, and it was undertaken under all sorts of pressure. For a start, *Dirty Mind* had sold less spectacularly than the eponymous debut album of Prince protégés The Time, who proceeded to upstage him night after night on the road. (There is a pretty complete consensus about this.) The band in the number two dressing room were garnering many of the best reviews. As with Rick James, the roots of Prince's deteriorating relationship with Morris Day – later dramatised in *Purple Rain* – were compounded by professional rivalry and a growing animosity towards anyone who did not see things his way. For Prince, for Warner, and for Steve Fargnoli's management team, the *Controversy* tour was a gamble against what looked like the most promising market demographic around, a melding of the r'n'b audience drawn to Day's group and a substantial white rock audience, a still uneasy coalition of heavy rock and guitar fans, punks and post-punks.

There had been a sharp warning the previous year when Prince had been booked to support the Rolling Stones, for two nights in L.A. The omens were good. Promoter Bill Graham was an industry legend; he was also the man who'd put Miles Davis on with white rock acts at the two Fillmores, East and West, heralding the trumpeter's crossover triumph. This was exactly the trajectory being mapped out for Prince – but that was jazz; this was showbiz.

Even if all the auguries seemed propitious, the outcome was bad and potentially disastrous. The nights of October 9 and 11, 1981, at the Memorial Coliseum were low points in Prince's early career. Bootlegs of both nights reveal a hostile crowd, booing what was presumably an unfamiliar repertoire and an unfamiliarly black sound. There nearly wasn't a second night. Prince fled the auditorium before the opening set was over and on the Saturday in between took sanctuary at home in Minneapolis. It took a measure of persuasion to fly him back to California for a second show that must have confirmed every one of his fears. This time, the crowd weren't merely hostile; they were armed. As soon as Prince and his musicians took the stage, they were pelted with fruit, lumps of rotten chicken, even bottles. One hefty one apparently struck new recruit Mark Brown.

The young bassist was the equivalent in Prince's band of Michael Henderson who'd given Miles Davis's fusion bands their raw, rock edge. He'd been recruited from Fantasy, another Minneapolis group, as a replacement for Andre Cymone. That relationship had taken some time to fall apart, presumably because of deep residual loyalties on both sides. Brown came in, though, at a time when Prince was changing, listening less to Twin Cities friends and much more to manager Steve Fargnoli. Like many artists convinced by their own publicity, Prince had become increasingly remote and egomaniacal.

The studied weirdness which had fuelled the publicity campaign for *Dirty Mind* now ran on its own momentum. Having given interviews to anyone willing to drop a dime, Prince now refused most offers. One trusted exception was Barbara Graustark of *Musician* magazine, who two years later, in another publication, *People's Weekly*, wrote the article that firmly cemented Prince's status as a self-determined outsider who deliberately flouted every remaining convention. As he became a personage and a (non-speaking) spokesman for amoral outlawry the band were just having fun. They were happy to join in pre-concert prayers – and there's every reason to think that Prince's insistence here was sincere – but as far as his increasingly apocalyptic take on ecstatic religion was concerned they were more hesitant. The Prince gospel was something akin to partying-as-prayer; the problem was he didn't practise it, even with his 'Uptown' friends. For the others, partying was enough. Prince's growing aloofness wasn't so much a Napoleon complex as a genuine dismay at his cohorts' enthusiasm for a rock 'n' roll lifestyle he seemed to profess only in metaphoric terms. They in turn can't be criticised too harshly. After several years' scuffling on the drab Twin Cities circuit, the band had been thrown into the big time. If they didn't buy into the full Prince philosophy, it's hard to imagine a group of black teenagers and early-twenty-year-olds who would.

There's some artistic evidence that Prince's isolation wasn't complete. The album that followed *Controversy* and established Prince as a radio-friendly crossover artist sounds much more of a band record than its predecessors, even if that impression only comes from the Sly Stone-influenced shared vocals of the title track. In 1982, it was time to party like it was already 1999.

6

The millennium came early to Uptown. The band stepped out like true believers to bear witness to a world turned upside-down. The sky was purple; people rushing everywhere; trying to run from the destruction; inhibitions finally overthrown in the vast carnival of hectic pleasure reflected in the soaring pop-funk of '1999'. It's hard to tell whether Prince is partying so hard he doesn't care, or whether Judgement Day really *is* a party.

He'd learned early the skill of using an album's first track to show his hand creatively: 'For You', the brilliant 'I Wanna Be Your Lover', 'Dirty Mind', and, less happily, 'Controversy'. The tone this time round is brilliantly summed up by Dave Hill as 'exquisite fatalism' and 'morbidly euphoric', though those descriptions work better for '1999' the track than for *1999* the album. The latter is a joyous sprawl, played out at considerable length and with a leaven of good-natured humour that could hardly be more different from the ludicrous petulance of its predecessor. Though not a concept album in the way *Purple Rain* was to be, *1999* feels like it might be the soundtrack to a show or an animated film, which is pretty much how Prince pitched it to Warner and to the band.

He's conspicuously absent from the front cover this time, though the name and title are both given in his own exuberant graphic, part childish graffiti, part Mati Klarwein nightmare, with a distinctly phallic cast to the numeral *1*. On the back cover, there he is with his paintbox and a sketchpad, naked under a satin sheet in a seducer's neon fantasy of a bedroom (with a 'C' moon peeping in the window). Prince stares suggestively at the camera, though this time the suggestion is that he might be about to draw the viewer rather than seduce her/him. Unless he already has; either way, it's a disturbingly intimate image and the fluorescent tubing round the room threatens to advertise the intimacy far and wide.

1999 was the album where Prince's technical skills caught up with his ambition. He has finally mastered his musical paintbox. The marriage of soul romance, r'n'b seduction and heavy metal apocalypse is consummated over eleven tracks of remarkable consistency. Gone is the fussy cross-brushing of the debut record and no place now for the raw, straight-from-demo feel of *Dirty Mind*. Even given the leeway he'd claimed from Warner, it was rare for black artists to be allowed to make double LPs. In fact *1999* is only three tracks longer than its predecessors and only really a single LP on which the longer cuts – 'D.M.S.R.', 'Automatic' and the epic 'Lady Cab Driver' – are spared an edit. When it failed to make much impact in Britain, it was reissued as a single disc, with three tracks dropped – 'International Lover', 'D.M.S.R.' and 'All the Critics Love U in New York' – rather than shortened. And yet, part of the album's success is its duration. Prince had always known how to ride a groove, James Brown-style; now he knew how to deliver it as well.

There are signs throughout that his approach has acquired a new sophistication. Though still largely dependent on drum machines, on 'Lady Cab Driver' he lays down a simple snareline instead, giving the rhythm a spanking physicality and suggesting that the eponymous heroine has shrewdly left the meter running as she's brought to orgasm by her passenger: a relatively undemanding vocal spot for another new protégé, Jill Jones. Prince had encountered her when she sang back-up vocals for Teena Marie, one of the support acts on the Rick James tour. Though later to be a tough-minded star in her own right, for the moment Jones's main duty was to sing side-stage on tour while Vanity 6 warmed up for Prince and The Time with a touch of burlesque.

It's hard to spot on the CD reissue and a casual glance at the original cover won't reveal it, largely because the writing is printed in reverse, but *1999* is for the first time attributed to Prince and the Revolution. Friends and associates – including Jimmy Jam and Dr Fink – remember their amazement when Prince came in carrying a tape, apparently put down only the night before, which turned out to be the instrumental for '1999'. This time, he opted not to multi-track his own vocals but to share the lead. This was not the original conception. A careful listen reveals that the melody changes with each line. This is because Prince had originally recorded a unison vocal, with himself leading and the others harmonising. In another intuitive decision, he decided to split the vocal, so what one hears from Jones, Dickerson and Lisa Coleman is actually a backing line promoted in the mix. Sharing the lead was a new approach for Prince, but it helped place the new single's apocalyptic message in a familiar rock context.

Backed with 'How Come U Don't Call Me Anymore', it reached number four in the rock and pop chart, his best showing since 'I Wanna Be Your Lover', three years earlier, and even made a preliminary dent on the British singles market, reaching number twenty-five. There were other strong contenders for single release on the album. 'D.M.S.R.' – Dance, Music, Sex, Romance – is a piece of engaging nonsense and might well have worked in edited form. Likewise, the longer still 'Automatic', though its clever dissection of sexual identities probably only works at full length. Prince asks us to consider whether love is glandular or spiritual, delivers his declaration in the same monotone he once applied to the 'Lord's Prayer' and does so over a machine beat which is the aural equivalent of *coitus inter-ruptus* or abrupt abstention. The ambiguity of the title is powerful and funny: are love and desire merely galvanic responses? Or, are our emotions merely 'automatic', rote reactions influenced by the conventions of popular song: 'U ask me if I love U; it's automatic / Cause everytime U leave me I die / That's automatic too.' As to the now familiar synthesis of sex and religion, the only uplift on offer here is take-off in a plane with the stewardesses (Lisa and Jill) coming on like a pair of dominatrixes. A similar take-off-and-landing conceit runs through 'International Lover', the album's final track and the climax of the *1999 ... show* (a better term than *live set*), during which Prince scaled a high onstage bed and fucked an unseen partner, if he wasn't merely pleasuring himself, which is equally possible given the album's narcissistic turn. *1999* saw him negotiate a complex transformation from lover to lover-and-beloved, an obscure object of desire as well as a walking phallic symbol.

Most of the album's songs were either too subtly ironic or too dependent on elaborate staging to work as singles, even with supporting visuals. In 1983, thanks to MTV's tacit colour bar, video still wasn't a priority for black acts. Prince also helped to change that. His choice of follow-up single was brilliant not just because it was a slice of unapologetic innuendo, but because it also turned him into a rock star and opened up the long-dreamed-of 'biracial' audience.

You don't need to have read twelve volumes of Sigmund Freud to understand 'Little Red Corvette', though the possibility that the singer is female makes for some interesting ambiguities. The song's cheerful amorality – 'It was Saturday night / I guess that makes it alright' – is wrapped around a slightly prissy disgust with the kinds of thing lust leads you to and the people it leads you to do it with. 'I guess I must be dumb / Cuz U had a pocket full of horses / Trojan and some of them used', 'Guess I should have closed my eyes / When U drove me to the place / Where your horses run free / Cuz I felt a little ill / When I saw all the pictures of the jockeys / That were there before me . . .' White rock 'n' roll generally avoided any hint of sexual anxiety, let alone references to used Trojans. Whatever the exact nature of the little red Corvette – cock or pussy – it was a far cry from Chuck Berry's wearily salacious 'My Ding-a-Ling', a feature of his stage act long before, somewhat edited, it became a surprise hit single.

Backed with the enigmatic 'All the Critics Love U in New York', which could almost have been written by a young black Truman Capote, 'Little Red Corvette' was a smash. It helped to break down the MTV barrier, only the second video to breach the station's unstated colour line. That was largely because Prince abandoned the oddly lumpy dancing of earlier promos and presented the Revolution as a real-life rock band, albeit one that had lifted the rock 'n' rollers' loud-stated ban on chicks. Prince and Dez cavorted like Mick and Keith, sharing a mic on the choruses, wielding guitars like true born axemen. Whatever audiences heard on *1999*, on 'Little Red Corvette' they saw a new rock god in the making.

Prince, though, aspired to the singleness of Jahweh; there were to be no other gods besides him, which meant that the writing was on the wall for Dickerson, as for most of the original entourage who had seen him through the difficult early years and the Stones debacle. The only exceptions were the female members of the group, presumably no threat to Prince's sexual vanity and a useful focus for his cross-dressing persona. Wendy Melvoin (daughter of jazz pianist Mike Melvoin) was drafted in on guitar to replace the departed Dez Dickerson, and another white girl, Lisa Coleman, had been brought aboard on keyboards. Both were accomplished musicians, with strong family backgrounds in pop. Later, Wendy's percussionist brother Jonathan would become part of the operation while twin sister Susannah joined as vocalist and enjoyed a passionate fling with the boss. Like Gayle Chapman, they brought a classical seriousness and a touch of glamour. They were also no immediate threat to Prince's leadership.

More important still to the Prince image was the all too accurately named Vanity 6, a female trio who gave a new and ironic twist to the term 'warm-up act'. Through no fault of Prince's, but thanks largely to unusually tramlined thinking at Warner, what might have been an interestingly satirical sidebar to the Prince phenomenon – the Chiffons' 'He's so Fine' reworked as 'He's so Dull' – ended up looking dull and exploitative; Vanity 6's 'Nasty Girl' is one of the low points in the royal canon. On stage, the trio was pure burlesque and you didn't have to be Andrea Dworkin to find their presentation offensive. By contrast, the suggestion that Wendy and Lisa – or 'Wendy & Lisa' as they came to be known inseparably when working as an independent unit

– might have a Sapphic side was handled with infinite subtlety. Compared to the blatancy of Vanity and Apollonia, they played the game of sexual ambiguity almost as well as Prince himself. And there was no doubting their importance to his creative vision. Fictionally, at least, they were to be cast as creators of his most famous song.

Prince himself had long since abandoned the panties and bandanna look in favour of sci-fi dandy, an extension of Jimi Hendrix's electric gypsy persona; it sat well with the rock stuff, and with the weirdly courteous rudeness of 'Let's Pretend We're Married': 'I want to fuck the taste out of your mouth'. It also gave a certain edge to the Oscar Wildeism of 'All the Critics Love U in New York'. More than one observer has pointed to the influence of Little Richard not just on Prince's piled-up bouffant hair (successor to his stature-enhancing Afro) but also on his projection of a confusingly aberrant sexuality. The dandy image also cements the curious amalgam of charm, violence, glamour, snobbery and *lèse-majesté* which fuels 'Lady Cab Driver'. In keeping with his gender-switching obsession, Prince reverses the roles in a familiar urban situation: female passenger has no cash, pays for trip with sexual favours. Prince takes his chauffeuse on the back seat and as she moans her way to climax, he dedicates each breathless thrust to someone or something in his personal demonology, including a brother lucky enough to have been born handsome and tall – Duane perhaps? It's an extraordinary performance, much as the coition seems to be, made all the stranger by the appearance on his moral shopping list of God and money, or rather the real biblical *radix malorum*, the love of money.

Cash was a constant issue, as it would be with Michael Jackson, who was about to upstage Prince with the success of *Thriller*, an album and video that helped to recalibrate music industry expectations later the same year as the *1999* tour. Prince kept his hinds on short commons. That was perhaps the only way he could control the burgeoning success of The Time, but he also applied it to loyal subjects like Denise/Vanity, who decided to quit at the end of the tour, disingenuously complaining that the boss was seeing other women but in reality convinced that she could make more money on her own. Her replacement was a lookalike Californian called Patricia Kotero. In his usual proprietorial way, Prince named her Apollonia (having presumably ruled out Lust, Greed and Envy as suitable stage-names) and, as if to underline the continuity, formed a group round her. Apollonia 6 was basically a rerun of Vanity 6, with the sacred/profane balance tweaked fractionally to the former. (No one has ever been clear why two trios were so named; the cynics' guess was that it referred to the number of nipples onstage, though one relatively informed observer suggests that the girls were presumed to have shadow-selves, sexual daemons representing their 'other' side.)

It was clear to all, and was made increasingly explicit by Prince himself, that they were starring in the movie of his life. As 1983 went on, it became clearer that the fantasy was about to be realised. Prince was now in a position to live his dreams. His new road manager was a direct link to one of his idols; Alan Leeds had been James Brown's guy; his brother Eric Leeds later became an important part of Prince's sound. After the histrionics (and for once the word means exactly what it should) of the *1999* tour, the logical next step was for Prince to become a movie star. His ambivalence about stage performance, honed by the Stones experience, sharpened by wayward musicians and technical gremlins, evaporated at the thought of multiple takes, perfect lighting and costume, and a firm directorial hand.

With *1999* Prince reinvented himself as an apocalyptic auteur. If Ike Turner and Erich von Stroheim had had a lovechild, he would have been the Prince of 1983. Withdrawn and cruel by turns, preaching freedom – the faux-gospel 'Free' is the forgotten track on *1999* – but wilfully denying it to his most loyal supporters, generous and mean by capricious turns, he was outwardly a success and inwardly trapped in the prism of his own ego. One line from 'Free' stands out in hindsight: 'Never let that lonely monster take control of U'. Lisa, Jill, Vanity and new keyboardist Wendy Melvoin all contributed to the backing vocals, possibly wondering if it applied to the man in front of them. The artistic licence of the Warner contract was coming home to roost. The tragicomedy of *The Rise and Fall of Ziggy Stardust and the Spiders from Mars*, another big influence, was being acted out for real.

Prince's personal isolation was guaranteed by the hiring

of the towering, bearded Chick Huntsberry as permanent bodyguard. At six foot six to Prince's five-foot-depends-on-the-heels, and better built for cracking heads than for getting down on his knees to pray with the rest of the group, Huntsberry seemed an unlikely acquisition. He was, however, impeccably rock 'n' roll and, after an uneasy start, impeccably obedient and can-do. Big Chick was around from the time of the *Controversy* tour but his media apotheosis was at the British Phonographic Industry show in 1985, where he escorted a now less than monosyllabic Prince to the podium to collect his award. Even after his departure from the entourage, Prince remained close to him and when Huntsberry died in 1990, arranged a benefit for his family.

The apocalypse of *1999* had been prefigured by a sky turned purple. The album had been made in a basement studio – known as 'Uptown' – at Prince's new mansion, just outside Minneapolis at Lake Minnetonka. It was heavily fenced off to deter visitors; it was also painted purple in case anyone missed who it belonged to, or mistook the signs of upward mobility. For the next few years, that same regal/phallic hue was to be Prince's signature colour as he alternated between the music pages and the gossip pages, almost always under headlines that punned 'rain' and 'reign'.

7

In 1956, Elvis Presley walked on to the set of *Love Me Tender* and began the second career that would take him to parts of the world and to an audience who would never see Elvis live. In 1953, seemingly dead and buried as a singer, Frank Sinatra had revived his career with a part in *From Here to Eternity*. Ever after, Sinatra balanced music and movie work with characteristic brilliance, using the camera, as he had the microphone, to project intimacy, anger, strength, vulnerability, sexual command and robust humour by turns, and always in one take. Parts ranged from demanding character roles to thinly reworked versions of Sinatra the entertainer, to roles that offered carefully ironised hints of other, darker associations. Sinatra both fuelled and protectively negated his own mythology by projecting it on a big screen.

By 1984, Prince was ready to do the same. He was still only an r'n'b star of the second rank, occasionally upstaged by his own entourage, and the victim of his own muddled press campaign, which seemed to alternate between saying too much – and too much that was untrue – and then saying nothing at all. To those around him, Prince had always seemed to be starring in the movie of his own life, self-cast as Greta Garbo. In line with the old Hollywood joke, though, having produced, arranged, composed and performed, Prince now wanted to *direct*. There had been no discernible narrative to the *1999* show, but it was clear that Prince was increasingly thinking in terms of scenarios. The cinema screen gives a new dimension not just to a tiny physical frame but to an ego as well. When it eventually emerged, the *Purple Rain* movie was a curious amalgam of auto-biography and fiction, oddly literal in places, blatantly self-aggrandising in others. At best it's a fudge, the darker elements of the original conception softened into sentimentality or slapstick, a searing plotline reduced to a series of album promos and iconic set pieces.

It very nearly didn't happen at all. The original scriptwriter, William Blinn – late forties, tough, white, ex-perienced – should have been inured to the tantrums of precocious children from his time as executive producer on *Fame*. In the event, he found Prince unmanageably prepos-terous and nearly abandoned the project when his star/auteur repeatedly walked out of meetings. He was, however, sufficiently intrigued and sufficiently convinced of the young man's talent to shape a script out of the dark materials he was given. It is well to keep the original back-story of *Purple Rain* in mind when watching the mish-mash of 'emotional biography' cobbled together by eventual scriptwriter and director Albert Magnoli. It's also worth pondering how very different a psychodrama and how much tougher a film might have resulted, perhaps something closer to Eminem's *Eight Mile*.

Prince's idea was that his character's parents should be killed at the beginning of the film, a classic murder-suicide with the anguished father turning the gun on himself after shooting his wife. As a premise, it's no more shocking, no more Oedipally freighted, if you give The Kid's mom and dad the names of John Nelson and Mattie Shaw. Knowing what their fictional fate might have been gives a disturbing edge – at least one part bathos – to the weary rowing that punctuates the film and to 'Francis''s eventual suicide attempt. It also blunts The Kid's lonely and arrogant pursuit of fame to know that instead of being violently orphaned he goes back to the family home and a cosy basement every night. Full of dolls and porcelain, Prince's lair looks more like a teenage girl's bedroom than a fully equipped seduction den. (It's hard not to make a comparison with another contemporary rock fantasy which treats family life as a faintly embarrassing irrelevance. *Wayne's World* disposes of parents and siblings simply by ignoring them. Given the date, it can be read as a wry commentary on the very different family romance of *Purple Rain*.)

Once the bleak original scenario – called *Dreams* – was thrown overboard, the only remaining psychological drama in *Purple Rain* is The Kid's emotional deadness. It's presumed to come from his unhappy home life but it lacks what drama critics would call a convincing objective correlative. It even *looks* wrong for a film that purports to tell a tale of obscurity to stardom. The leading man is clearly a star right from the off, and equally clearly not prepared to re-enact his callow younger self. The callowness comes through, nonetheless. Prince has a certain genius as a poseur, and severe limitations as an actor, as he was to prove again in *Under the Cherry Moon*. His most effective narratives are almost always still photographs, like those taken by Allen Beaulieu but carefully assembled and art-directed by himself. The energy and charisma he projects as a live performer disappear when he switches to scripted action. This much was evident from early videos, where even the dancing is clumsy and self-conscious. It's still more so in *Purple Rain*.

The two main story strands are his pursuit of Patricia Kotero/Apollonia and his musical rivalry with another of the bands who play at the First Avenue club. The first is languid, knowing, almost entirely devoid of sexual tension, an unembarrassed slice of rock video chauvinism. The second, which was bitter and vicious in Blinn's first draft, is played for laughs, largely thanks to Morris Day's clowning as the so-cool-your-teeth-will-chatter super dude who fronts the rival group. (For all their on- and off-camera rivalry, Day would continue to figure in Prince's life. The Time are strongly featured on *Graffiti Bridge*, where Day also gets behind the drums on 'New Power Generation'. His acting career took off with a part in the ABC sitcom *New Attitude*.)

The real dramas of *Purple Rain* are slightly harder to decode. In a film that places enormous symbolic importance on colour, skin pigment is the most striking signifier. Unlike Michael Jackson, Prince surrounds himself with white faces. Apart from Day and Clarence F. Williams III, who plays his father, most of the principal actors are Caucasian. The mother is played by Olga Kartalos, a Greek actress. The only member of Prince's/The Kid's band not prominently featured is bassist Mark Brown, who was presumably on his way out anyway; his token appearance only underlining the vanilla flavour of the rest, his new name Brown Mark almost crudely dismissive. Stalwarts Matt Fink and Bobby Z are mostly silent presences, but Wendy and Lisa are cast as the agents of The Kid's epiphany. For the purposes of the story at least, they are the writers of 'Purple Rain' itself. As will be seen in the next chapter, collaboration plays an important though sometimes ambiguous part in Prince's career. Here, it's turned into the major plot device. The film's dramatic and musical climax is The Kid's surrender to the inevitability of working with others, sharing a vision, accepting that his is not the only functioning imagination in this universe.

* * *

Offstage, The Kid's sound-world isn't much more convincing than his interior design. His choice of make-out music is a tape of a crying girl, played backwards. It fits in with the weeping dove symbolism of the film's and album's second most famous song, but it's an odd gesture and incongruous enough to disturb – or at least perturb – the otherwise pliant Apollonia. It is, admittedly, the kind of thing a nerdily clever, socially gauche adolescent might lay on to impress a girl, but with all the psychological realism sucked out of Blinn's original script, all that is left is two young and very knowing adults playing at a form of sexual innocence possibly alien to them both, or certainly left far behind.

There is another element to The Kid's 'growth', an awkward parallelism between his father's brooding violence and his own casually diffident mistreatment of women. In one notorious incident, he persuades Apollonia to dive fully clothed into a lake; instead of joining her, Prince rides off on his motorcycle. It would have disturbed the feminist lobby less if she'd lost her cool instead of smiling indulgently.

The sheer strangeness of their courtship – a mixture of romantic cliché and soft porn – almost suggests the antics of two young Martians brought up on a diet of films found in a canister sent out by a doomed earth. The affectless oddity of manners, contextless streets, soaked-in colour, as well as the relentless message of the lyrics suggested that the apocalypse promised in '1999' had already taken place and that it wasn't half as bad as 'Downtown' feared, an eruption of sensation that had shorted out ordinary feeling as well as moral convention. Not the smallest sign of Prince's international apotheosis in the aftermath of *Purple Rain* was that *Pravda* picked him out in late 1984 as the latest symptom of American youth's hedonistic nihilism.

Ever blind to the beam in its own eye, the Soviet government paper wondered at the veneration accorded this tiny black mote with a guitar who seemed to represent himself as the other pillar of capitalist decadence: Jesus Christ. A nation that embalms and makes auto-icons of its leaders shouldn't be throwing the first stone, but for a bunch of atheistic dialectical materialists, the Russians were very quick to spot the religious dimension of Prince's mission. It was made explicit in one of the songs on *Purple Rain*. 'Die' probably has an Elizabethan second, sexual meaning in the lyric – like 'come' and 'high' in a Doors song – but 'I Would Die 4 U' also cast Prince as a Christ-like saviour, while 'Take Me With U', a duet with Apollonia, hints at a kind of nirvana in sex. There are other themes in play, but the overwhelming atmosphere of *Purple Rain* is a post-apocalyptic libertinism.

Unlike the usual run of popular music films, anything from *42nd Street* to *Eight Mile* and maybe taking in *Bird* along the way, there's no sense in *Purple Rain* that The Kid is ever anything but a star, not just in his own head, but in reality, or at very least the hectic reality of his peers. At home, The Kid may simply be a kid again, but even his attempts to separate his warring parents look perfunctory and petulant, prompted by jealousy rather than righteous anger. His isolation and self-doubt are dealt with only erratically, as in the device of Wendy & Lisa being the composers of 'Purple Rain' itself, and the climactic 'Baby, I'm a Star', supposedly the apotheosis of a new rock god, is distinctly anticlimactic.

* * *

Movie culture arguably has a broader cultural leverage than pop music, which still tends to be demographically (and often ethnically) segmented, and it was the movie of *Purple Rain* that propelled Prince into the cultural mainstream. For all its limitations, it's a revealing artefact, but it's the album that stands up better twenty years on. Less original, less dramatic than *Dirty Mind*, and it might be argued that Prince never again made anything as sheerly powerful as his third album, it's a curious mixture of bombast and delicacy, a triumphant realisation of the 'biracial' sound he's been sketching in since 'I'm Yours' and eventually pulled off on *1999*. The songs veer between bubblegum romance and sexual grind on one axis, flagrant originality and magpie eclecticism on another.

The set begins, significantly, with Prince in preacher mode, intoning an idiosyncratic version of the 'Dearly beloved' address that precedes a wedding. There is no mistaking that what follows is to be a form of ritual as well as theatre, but one subsumed under the hectic fatalism – 'we're all gonna die' – of Prince's lyric. 'Let's Go Crazy' isn't the obvious opening hymn, but it cements from the very beginning the album's air of amoral celebration and doomed pleasure. Musically, it's the natural successor to 'Little Red Corvette' and very much in the same mould, though it wasn't until February 1985 and the run-up to *Around the World in a Day* that the track was released as a single. There was at least one stronger, if less obvious, contender on the album.

'Take Me With U' follows and as if to clinch the proof of his ability to write strong generic pop songs, Prince follows it with the moodily romantic 'The Beautiful Ones', which betrays a strong influence from British New Romanticism. 'Computer Blue' is a strange, two-part idea, co-written with Wendy & Lisa, and musically from a very different place to everything else on the album, though one can imagine a young man capable of listening to backwards tapes of a girl crying having a hand in this kind of experimentalism. It would be a dull track if it were sequenced with another ten tracks like it. Here, it stands out as the work of an artist who chooses – for the moment at least – not to be imprisoned by a style.

Lest anyone thought he was having what twenty years later would have been identified as 'a Radiohead moment', Prince followed up 'Computer Blue' (a jazz-tinged John Nelson idea) with the savage 'Darling Nikki', a cold, snarling punk-funk anthem in which Nikki is presented 'masturbating with a magazine'. The only 18-certificate moment on the whole album, delivered to the jogging, nursery-rhyme beat which often conceals Prince's most powerful songcraft, it's the meanest, almost the basest track in the Prince canon, but as ever it conceals a surprise. Buried away, almost inaudible in its raunchy instrumental, is a vocal line played wrong way round which deciphers as 'Hello, how are you? I'm fine, because I know the Lord is coming soon, coming, coming soon'. That backwards tape he played Apollonia offered a clue that there was going to be more to these songs than met the eye. Startling as its mix of profane and sacred is, the other great coup of 'Darling Nikki' is its brilliant positioning on the album. It's separated from the ambiguous closing sequence that presents Prince as Jesus Christ, Black Superstar – 'I Would Die 4 U', 'Baby, I'm A Star' and 'Purple Rain'; all recorded live at First Avenue during a preview – by one of the most remarkable records in the history of pop.

With its haunted, pleading vocal, 'When Doves Cry' is a genuine *cri de coeur*, saturated with emotion and delivered without a shred of irony. The sly pomp, disposable romance and vicious cleverness that defines the rest of the album is missing at its centre. Whether or not it is autobiographical, the references to family – 'Maybe I'm just like my father', 'Maybe I'm just like my mother' – make it seem so, and that's an impression the movie was guaranteed to reinforce. Musically, it's astonishing, not least because Prince dispensed with a bassline altogether, virtually unheard of in black music, accompanying his vocal with sparse keyboard stabs and a trademark Linn drum track which has been processed and thickened. Prince's gospelly wails are the only other embellishment.

Released on May 16, 1984, 'When Doves Cry' spent five

weeks at the top of the *Billboard* pop charts, eight at the top of the black chart. In terms of musical 'biracism', this was exceptional, even in a market that had been transformed by Michael Jackson's *Thriller*, released in December 1982. Unlike the legendary Jon Landis-directed video for Jackson's title track, the promo for 'When Doves Cry' was a collage of scenes from the forthcoming movie, cleverly self-reinforcing publicity for the album and film which followed in the release schedule at the end of June and July respectively. *Purple Rain* was also Prince's first number one album, outselling everything else for nearly six months. The majority of black music fans remained – perforce but also from aesthetic loyalty – devoted to their vinyl albums, but a new white, middle-class audience also had the disposable income for a new technology. *Purple Rain* was the first time Prince had been heard on CD, whose hard, clear sound suited perfectly a song like 'When Doves Cry'.

The demographics were working at last, and so was the symbolism: what better image for a rock messiah than a weeping dove? And what more potent sign of his Christ-like nature than that his greatest triumph should be signalled by his greatest sorrow? The song's musical uniqueness helped reinforce Prince's divided nature: carnal and spiritual, defeated and triumphal, solitary and suddenly at the head of a popular mass. It was a position that would define and haunt him in the years ahead.

8

If Prince's carefully confected image was polymorphous, so were his creative energies. The Prince story cannot satisfactorily be told in terms of his recording and performing career alone. Certainly before it, but even after the global success of *Purple Rain*, a substantial proportion of his working time was always devoted to other performers, sometimes altruistically, often proprietorially, his presence most often pseudonymous but so transparently that no one was misled for long. Aware that the market would only support so much Prince product, he poured himself into any number of side projects.

One argument suggests that the flipside of Prince's Napoleon complex is a disinterested generosity; another, more caustic line insists that his support of other acts was mere empire-building and his transparent anonymity the sign of a Machiavellian *eminence grise* – or *eminence pourpre*. There is no mistaking how differently Prince treated male and female associates – Morris Day and The Time, say, as against Jill Jones, Vanity or Apollonia – but it's too easy to suggest that while the boys represented a challenge to the alpha male, the women were always willing to play handmaidens to the godhead. The boys were always boys in Prince's world, cocky show-offs who could be reined in whenever they showed signs of walking the walk as well, as happened to The Time, Dez Dickerson and Mark Brown.

The women generally enjoyed a less stinting patronage, but again either because Prince enjoyed the idea, and still more the reality, of running a stable of beautiful starlets, and presenting them in demeaningly sexual roles, or because Jill, Wendy & Lisa, Sheila E later, and even Vanity and Apollonia allowed him to project aspects of his own femininity. Even if one veers to the former view, it's striking how often Prince's women are cast in sadomasochistic roles, stripping and 'whipping' the boss, strapping him in for some much needed discipline in 'Automatic' or exchanging the kind of knowing glances, as Wendy & Lisa often do, which suggests that they, not he, are in charge. Much depends on individual experience or on a settled conviction about Prince's real nature, if there is such a thing beyond the prisms of image.

* * *

Dolly Parton may have declined the offer of a Prince song but over the years some of his greatest and presumably most lucrative successes have been from songs performed by other artists. Even if Prince had remained an unseen songwriter, with no public profile of his own, he would still be remembered for the impact he made on the pop charts in the 1980s and 1990s. It squares very much with his idiosyncratic take on femininity – *not* in a form Dolly Parton would have understood or approved – that the majority of artists who dipped into the Prince songbook were women.

Unless 'she' really is an actual person, one of Prince's most intriguing alter egos is 'Camille'. The name is credited on *Sign 'O' The Times* as lead singer on 'Strange Relationship' and 'If I Was Your Girlfriend' and joint lead with Sheena Easton on 'U Got the Look'. No one has ever seriously doubted that 'Camille' *is* Prince. 'She' is the only guest artist not thanked in the closing credits and there *he* is on the video to 'U Got the Look', playing out the song's puzzling ethnic drama. Even so, it's tempting to think that Prince or someone close to him had a hand in allowing the bootleg *Camille* to escape from Paisley Park, as if she had a separate existence.

Easton is a fascinating figure in recent pop history. Romantically linked to Prince, and if the tabloids are further to be believed, the recipient of a love-token in the shape of a Parisian apartment, she was already the perfect pop confection. A former trainee teacher, Easton was groomed for stardom by one of the earliest wannabe programmes of British television, *Big Time*, hosted by Esther Rantzen. She scored a hit with '9 to 5' (*not* the Dolly Parton song from the film of that name, and for that reason later retitled 'Morning Train' in the US), in whose video she appeared as a funky young housewife, cheerily vacuuming the carpet while hubby was out at the office. It's a wry, pre-post-feminist take on Burt Bacharach's 'Wives and Lovers'.

Prince clearly didn't see Easton in this role at all, even ironically. The song he wrote for her, as 'Alexander Nevermind', is that very rare thing in the pop of the time, a frank exploration of female sexuality shorn of romance. 'Sugar Walls' is cheerfully unambiguous and coupled with press reports of their affair, if such it was, it recast Easton as a cock-loving siren. Even in retrospect, it makes Kylie Minogue's similar makeover look tame, and it propelled Easton into an improbable new career, even at one stage playing the part of Don Johnson's ill-fated wife in *Miami Vice*. She and Prince wrote some songs together during their romance, of which 'The Arms of Orion' from the *Batman* soundtrack is probably the best. Long before he married Mayte Garcia, Prince had always liked to create the impression that female band members were lovers, too. British soul singer Mica Paris, who met and worked with Prince later in the decade, suggests that most of the rumours are simply that; 'We weren't as good friends as the papers made out.'

He certainly was 'good friends' with percussionist Sheila E. The daughter of Santana percussionist Pete Escovedo, she met Prince some time during the making of *For You*, presumably impressing him by her closeness to one of his idols as well as by her musical pedigree. Like many of the women who came within his orbit, though more independently than most, Sheila had ambitions towards a solo career.

An early pair of album projects, *Sheila E in The Glamorous Life* in 1984 and the later *Sheila E in Romance 1600*, are presented as movies, a very 'Prince' approach and doubly so given the carefully posed monochrome cover of the earlier record. In this case, his presence is more as influence than intervention. For the second album, Prince co-wrote 'A Love Bizarre', a title which would have recalled Coltrane's *A Love Supreme* to two jazz-aware musicians. Otherwise, it seems to have been a relationship of equals. Sheila E later became a ranking member of Prince's touring group, and one of his most effective stage foils.

* * *

Wendy Melvoin and Lisa Coleman are among Prince's most intriguing former associates. Loyal to the point of folly, they found themselves tightly woven into his harem-fantasies and yet managed to maintain an impressive independence of thought. Recognising that he had become perhaps too dependent on their input, or having absorbed it to his own satisfaction, Prince fired them midway through the recording of the abortive *Dream Factory*. One track, 'Power Fantastic', appeared on Prince's greatest hits compilation, partly because it was already well known as a bootleg. The circumstances of recording had been bizarre, with Lisa Coleman (also shortly to go) playing her piano part in an upstairs room, while the rest of the band gathered in the studio.

Unlike many of his former male associates, Wendy and Lisa seemed to come out of the relationship relatively unbruised. They recorded three better than average albums for Columbia and Virgin, before a fourth project disappeared into the cracks in the release schedule, whereupon they became a pair of vaguely feminist fixers, appearing in some capacity on records by Joni Mitchell and Me'shell Ndegeocello, and writing film music. Their standard line now is that a reunion with Prince isn't out of the question – he kept the lines open with a dedication on *Emancipation* to them – but only if he picks up the phone.

* * *

'Sugar Walls' isn't the best context for a pitch at Prince-the-feminist, but underneath the proprietorial swagger there has always been something impressively disinterested in Prince's sponsorship of women friends and fellow performers. A similar track title appears on Jill Jones's eponymous 1987 album, which Prince helped to write and produce. Co-written with Jones, 'G Spot' is a funkier, less poppy song than 'Sugar Walls'. It may seem like further leering on Prince's part, but his role in Jones's career was notably generous: he even offered to remove his name from the credits entirely, not to disown the record, but so that Jones would receive full recognition for it. Even so, the whole pitch of the album, and relentless press questioning of Jones about her exact relationship with Prince – which she always maintained was professional, friendly and sisterly – guaranteed that everyone heard it, subliminally at least, as part of the Prince *oeuvre*.

If the possibility of a feminist Prince seems so remote as to be laughable, it is possible to claim him for post-feminism, or at least as an early influence on the sexually aware female songwriting of the 1990s. Jones's baby-doll voice – a version of Prince's own falsetto – is palpably self-aware, just as her presentation on the debut album's cover as a knowing woman-child is so obviously a self-chosen pose rather than an imposed image. Jones's album is clever, satirical (she clearly doesn't buy the mechanical liberation of the whole G-spot debate), and musically subtle. Smart as she is, someone else has to be given much of the credit. Arguably the most convincing contemporary equivalent of Prince is Missy Elliott, whose influence in the studio and as a writer is almost greater than her performing presence.

* * *

At the turn of the 1990s, Prince put enormous energy – and a substantial tranche of Paisley Park's dwindling assets – into the career of Cincinatti rapper Carmen Electra. He had initially approached her with the idea of forming another girl band along the lines of Apollonia/Vanity 6 but with an eye to the burgeoning hip-hop market. What the normally astute Prince was last to appreciate was, as his marketing department and the pluggers who tried to sell her eponymous

1993 album must have tried to tell him, that her pneumatic talents were probably better suited to the camera. Electra later became a *Playboy* model, calendar girl and host of an MTV dating show.

It's ironic that an album by Rosie Gaines, who with all due respect is better served keeping her clothes on, but who can sing like Aretha Franklin, should have been shelved during Prince's dispute with Warner. Justice might have reversed the situation, though posterity has effectively 'disappeared' Electra's lame effort.

* * *

The brightly coloured pop rainbow that followed *Purple Rain* was the most obvious sign of Prince's still developing promise as a songwriter. Though there have been resurgences of interest since, the mid-1980s were a highpoint. 'Nothing Compares 2 U' was a massive video hit for Sinéad O'Connor, with whom Prince was not on good terms. It was, though, originally written for Susannah Melvoin. In 1986, having apparently run into Prince while flying between gigs, The Bangles had a massive hit with the chipper psychedelia of 'Manic Monday'. Ostensibly written by 'Christopher Tracy' (a first appearance for the character who appears on that year's *Parade*), it was previously recorded by Apollonia 6, but even if it hadn't been it's instantly recognisable as a Prince song, based once again on the '1999' riff.

Some years later, a flagging career (or possibly two) was

given a substantial fillip when the redoubtable Tom Jones collaborated on a version of one of the standout tracks from *Parade*. So important a part did 'Kiss' play in Jones's revival as a credible rocker that The Art of Noise's role in the single was quickly forgotten. It remains a surprisingly rare example of a male artist picking up a Prince song. Apart from The Time (whose subordinate status is underlined by the title of their third album *Ice Cream Castles*, the Joni Mitchell reference very much a Prince gesture) and the by then estranged Andre Cymone, who used 'The Dance Electric' on his ill-starred solo *A.C.*, little of Prince's work for others was given a male voicing. He did, however, form The Family as a front band. Again either selflessly or mischievously, Prince credits all the songs on the 'group''s eponymous 1985 debut to Jerome Benton, Jellybean Johnson, Eric Leeds and Susannah Melvoin (all identified simply by the first names) and casting Paul 'St Paul' Peterson as the lead singer. Nonetheless, the songwriting is unmistakably his and he plays virtually all the instruments.

* * *

There have always been stories and rumours about possible Prince collaborations. Michael Jackson – or producer/arranger Quincy Jones – apparently offered him a lead vocal spot on *Bad*, but Prince turned it down, largely because he wasn't having his greatest rival snarl 'Your butt is mine' at him in the very first line of the title song. He also seems to have backed out of a suggested pairing with Miles Davis, who perhaps remembering his abortive association with Jimi Hendrix spent his last decade scouting pop and soul concerts for fresh material and new faces. Miles apparently regarded Prince as the real thing – his 'Duke Ellington of the '80s' is a shrewd characterisation – and responded enthusiastically when he was sent some instrumental tapes and a vocal coyly entitled 'Can I Play With U?' (also included was a note signed 'God', which would have tickled the trumpeter). Miles overdubbed his own trumpet part and had the track slated for inclusion on *Tutu*, when Prince recalled it, ostensibly because he wasn't satisfied with its quality. Shortly before Miles died, he played at Prince's Glam Slam club in Minneapolis, but the proprietor refused to go on stage. The two did play together on Chaka Khan's *CK* album and did once appear together at Paisley Park, but the audience were wealthy Christmas party-goers raising money for underprivileged children.

Prince has also flirted with Madonna, who with Jackson is the only other star of comparable magnitude in the period, but compared to both of them a model of career longevity. It seems she suggested some merger of Paisley Park with her own Maverick operation. He has also recorded, but not released, a cover of her 'Like a Prayer'. Prince was doubtless fascinated by Madonna's unabashed but carefully airbrushed take on sexuality. Working with women and on 'female' themes continued to be his staple, though mostly with singers who didn't threaten his ascendancy.

In 1983, he co-wrote 'Stand Back' with Stevie Nicks for her album *The Wild Heart*, and a decade later 'Why Should I Love You?' for Kate Bush's *The Red Shoes*. However, once Prince had established Paisley Park and its business arm PRN – for Prince Rogers Nelson – he was much freer to sign acts and shape their careers in the way he had The Time and The Family. PRN is a famously reticent organisation but it has made a notably generous contribution to not a few musical careers, promoting acts who never seemed likely to be more than musically interesting loss-leaders. Given how domineering a producer/A&R man he could be, there is an impressive level of disinterest. Even when there was a whiff of nepotism, Prince put his considerable creative presence behind the project, as when he wrote and produced nearly all of future wife Mayte's *Children of the Sun* (coyly switching the gender on 'The Most Beautiful Boy in the World'). He made a Paisley Park star out of gospeller Mavis Staples and expanded the label's eclectic jazz-funk-fusion roster with former DJ Taja Sevelle, who'd had a walk-on part in *Purple Rain* and contributed a backing vocal to 'The Ladder'. Perhaps remembering his own precocious debut, he also gave a leg-up to thirteen-year-old Tevin Campbell who in a familiar analogy had been identified as the new Stevie Wonder and the new Michael Jackson, a potent trading line at a time when the present Michael Jackson was looking and sounding a bit shop soiled. Others include Elisa Fiorillo, Ingrid Chavez and Paula Abdul, all relatively undemanding singers. More complex was Parliament guru George Clinton's association with Paisley Park. Though he shared some of Prince's lineage – James Brown and Sly Stone – but with the cosmic theatre of the Sun Ra Arkestra thrown in, Clinton took a much more political view of black funk and was mystified, not to say disturbed, by Prince's apparent quietism.

He made a minor rap star out of Carmen Electra, before she went on to fame as a centrefold and calendar girl, and gave saxophonist Candy Dulfer a secure footing for her pop-jazz approach with the touching imprimatur 'When I want sax I send for Candy'. And he continued to use songwriting for others as an outlet for some transgressive role-playing. Songs like 'Baby Go-Go' (another 'Joey Coco' composition) helped give Nona Hendryx's *Female Trouble* disc that same ambiguously gendered quality Prince was projecting in his own work. But they also demonstrated how much more comfortably he inhabited different song styles – bubblegum pop, soul, soul-rock, r'n'b – when those styles didn't have to sit shoulder to shoulder on a Prince album. Having gone multi-platinum and in the process broken down a deep and long-standing racial split in the pop audience, Prince had to wonder where his own records were going to head next.

9

If Prince's utopian/dystopian Uptown was originally conceived as a dark urban stew, defined by aggressive libertinism and ghetto politics, the next album transformed it into a curious psychedelic paradise called Paisley Park. The change of location and mood, which must have alarmed the Warner executives who attended the tapes' ritual unveiling, is marked by a new sound-world, into which flute, violin, oud and darbuka all make an unexpected entry, and which dispenses to a degree with the synthesized drums which had been such a distinctive aspect of Prince's music. For the first and only time in Prince's career, the electric guitar is not emphasised, sometimes omitted in favour of piano, and rarely distorted. The atmosphere is muted, and wry rather than sardonic, the eroticism low-key, the politics utopian rather than apocalyptic. In production values and sound-world, it might almost be a Beatles album.

Released in April 1985, *Around the World in a Day* is not just the first record to be released under his own Paisley Park imprint (still part of the Warner family) but ironically given later statements the first record on which the members of The Revolution play a full collaborative part. That's partly because much of the material was worked up, not by Prince alone in his Lake Minnetonka fortress, but by the whole band during rehearsals for the marathon *Purple Rain* tour. The chronology is important. Talking to *Rolling Stone*, Prince suggested that moving on to the new album so quickly was in retrospect a smart move: 'I didn't wait to see what happened with *Purple Rain*. That's why the two albums sound completely different.' Had he or The Revolution known then how unprecedently successful the album and tour were going to be (a gross of $22 million in the latter case), there might have been more pressure to make *Purple Rain Mk II*. Might have been, were not the leader gripped by a hex that insisted on unpredictable novelty: 'It's almost like a curse 2 know U can always make something new,' as he expressed it later. Consciously or unconsciously, Prince was echoing Miles Davis's often-quoted (and in his case misleading) claim, 'I have to change. It's like a curse.'

Like Miles, Prince often signalled a new direction with a radical shift in his cover art. Doug Henders's surreal montage marks a 180-degree turn away from Allan Beaulieu's stark monochrome but also from the steam and neon of *Purple Rain*. The Revolution are portrayed as a gentle tribe, living out an idyll under cotton-candy clouds. The female form is celebrated, but this time almost subliminally in the outlines of an anthropomorphic landscape. The brutal nihilism of past records is replaced by a gentler transcendence: a stepladder rises out of a wave-lapped pool and into the sky. This was the symbolism Prince chose to clothe himself in when he turned to video direction for the first time. 'The Ladder' is also there among the songs, a quiet, gnomic harbinger of the plainer religiosity of 'The Cross' on *Sign 'O' The Times*.

It has always been difficult to decode Prince's spiritual beliefs. Before his apparent conversion to the Jehovah's Witnesses in the 1990s and the quoting of the New World Edition of the Bible in the lyrics to *The Rainbow Children*, Prince had moved from a relatively conventional background to an eclectic, some might say pragmatic, exploration of world faiths. Certainly, Prince had a church-going childhood and when he married Mayte Garcia on St Valentine's Day in 1996 the ceremony was conducted by the Rev. Keith Johnson at Park Avenue Methodist United Church in Minneapolis. Other rumours suggested that he was studying Buddhism, and as discussed above the photographic artwork on *Prince* is seemingly influenced by Hindu imagery. On *Emancipation*, he toys with Egyptian eschatology.

Like John Coltrane's on *A Love Supreme*, which refers to a supreme being but not to an obviously Christian God or Jesus Christ, Prince's brand of spiritualism is knowingly eclectic and individualistic. Immediately after 'The Ladder', there's a glimpse of the old, unregenerate Prince, a reminder that the album's Summer of Love aura is little more than a front. 'Temptation' is nicely placed at the very end of *Around the World in a Day* to wrong-foot any listener naive enough to think that the libertine has fallen for the comfortable illusion of romantic love. During the song, Prince disputes with the deity, though this God sounds very much like his own octave-shifted superego. For the most part, though, it's generic dirty funk, with a trademark guitar part.

Taken together, 'The Ladder' and 'Temptation' are Prince's most explicit statement of the sacred–profane dichotomy, with profanity a clear winner. An album that starts out sounding like a deliberate attempt to avoid the sound-world of *Purple Rain* evolves into its natural successor. However 'different', read 'eccentric', it must have seemed to the executives invited to the pastel-themed playthrough at Warner in New York, and to the fans who bought *Around the World in a Day* in steadily decreasing numbers after its release in April 1985, it also carries a few worrying hints of musical self-parody among its elaborate homages. To stick with the problematic side two of the LP for the moment, there is no mistaking what is being beaten in 'Tambourine' and it isn't just sheepskin and bells. Here the drums are live (played by Prince himself) and prominent, but the track has a cobbled-together feel. Straight after 'Tambourine' comes 'America', a strange patriotic anthem in which one searches in vain for the least hint of irony. After that, and coming just before the 'Ladder'/'Temptation' finale, is 'Pop Life', which is by contrast either deeply ironic or similarly literal, perhaps a dig at the way fellow musicians like to primp their vanity by powdering their noses or else a chastened celebration of the way pop music and

A rare keyboard shot – the teenage Prince in 1977, in ecstatic
Stevie Wonder pose.

Musical bi-racism: the album and film that redefined 'crossover' success.

Rock Dionysus – late '80s.
© Corbis, photographer: Neil Preston

Suit, tie, microphone – just a singer with his band – Prince and the Revolution, May 1986.

© Corbis, photographer: Roger Ressmeyer

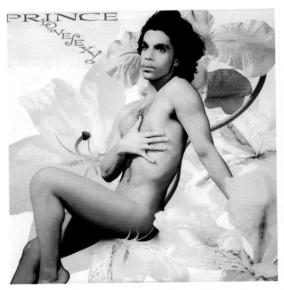

The Puck of popular music, but did another scandalous cover deflect appreciation of fine music?

Roll-neck, chalk stripes, a pretty ordinary guitar – the musician grows up.

© Pace Gregory/Corbis Sygma

The Artist, on a plinth of his own design – Madison Square
Garden, September 1998.

© Corbis, photographer: Mitchell Gerber

The most beautiful girl in the world – Prince and Mayte towards the end.

© *Getty, photographer: Sinead Lynch*

Thoughtful. Prince in 2004.
© *Corbis, photographer: Lucy Nicholson/Reuters*

star gossip help relieve the quiet desperation of ordinary American lives. In or out of album context, it's a curious song and a hard one to read.

Side one of the LP is an entirely different matter. It contains one of Prince's most perfect pop songs, the Beatles- and Joni-influenced 'Raspberry Beret', but also the plain weird 'Condition of the Heart', a piece so insubstantial it makes thistledown seem leaden. (Around this time, Joni acknowledged her influence on Prince: specifically his use of the unorthodox harmonies generated by her guitar tunings.) Jonathan Melvoin plays tambourine on 'Around the World in a Day', a song written by Lisa's brother David Coleman and then tinkered with by Prince and John Nelson. This is truly a family affair, a creative commune in which Prince can briefly pose as first among equals. 'Paisley Park' has a similar structure to the title track and the same almost folksy feel, but the song which was to define Prince's new imaginative abode (and give its name to his recording studio and new Camelot) works better as an instrumental, which is how it appeared on the 12" release, than as a lyric. The words are preposterous; a sign, perhaps, that Prince's often shaky, often perverse ability to verbalise his ideas was faltering, or taking second place to straight musicianship.

His most explicit namecheck of The Beatles was the title of *The Black Album*, the notorious 'bootleg' which supposedly referenced the Fab Four's so-called *White Album* (actually just called *The Beatles*), but it was widely thought at the time that *Around the World in a Day* was a deliberate effort to emulate Lennon and McCartney's songcraft. If so, the model wasn't *Sgt Pepper's Lonely Hearts Club Band*, as usually assumed, but *A Magical Mystery Tour*. The album's polystylistic oddity – black church euphoria to gossamer pop to hard funk – calls for a connecting narrative more than The Beatles' flawed experiment did, and more than *Purple Rain* did. Listeners wondered what was going on in Prince's head, a question that became increasingly rhetorical as its contents got ever more muddled in the years ahead.

* * *

As well as flagging up his spiritual and religious concerns, hinting at a more humble and less sensual route to transcendence, 'The Ladder' also became an important symbol of Prince's complex professional evolution. Not for him a terse press release. Instead, Prince announced that his next transition would take place on the final night of the ongoing *Purple Rain* tour, at Miami on April 7, 1985. Even those unaware of the star's Messiah complex could not have missed the significance of the date. Prince chose Easter Sunday to announce that he was retiring, and in the process dissolving the Revolution. He told his manager that he was 'going to look for the ladder', presumably to move on up to some higher celestial realm. It didn't happen, of course, but Prince had learned the market value of such gestures. He wanted to shrug off The Kid the way David Bowie had sloughed off his Ziggy Stardust character.

Prince also told Fargnoli, 'Sometimes it snows in April', which might just mean 'Shit happens' or might contain some recognition that The Revolution and the whole *Purple Rain* phenomenon might be terminating before its due time. The unseasonal frost actually caught *Around the World in a Day*, which only managed three weeks at the top of the *Billboard* chart, though it lingered in the low numbers for most of the rest of 1985.

* * *

Purple Rain had managed to keep Bruce Springsteen's *Born in the USA* off the top of the album charts for twenty weeks. While in reality all this meant was that one brand of irony was selling better than another, it was widely taken as a sign that wholesome working-class values and a ruggedly untroubled sexuality were losing out (in rock at least, but who knew, perhaps throughout society?) to perversity and decadence. (Prince has always enjoyed a deeply ambivalent press; 'His Royal Badness' was also, more sourly, the 'Purple Pain' and 'Ponce'.) The tabloids made hay with his diminutive stature, effeminate appearance and tantrums, though they must have been aware that Prince effortlessly lured attractive women (and white women at that) away from substantially taller and more conventionally handsome men. When stereotypes collided with his own ambivalent presentation, the media began to portray Prince as a paranoid recluse, conducting all manner of unseemly saturnalia behind the closed gates of his mansion and in a series of tour hotels. Particularly treasured was his silent appearance at the 1985 British Phonographic Awards, one of the first fruits of international success after *Purple Rain*. Prince stepped out to collect his award in his flounciest clothes, fluttering his eyelashes like Gloria Swanson, and accompanied by the musclebound six-foot-six minder Chick Huntsberry whose central role in the life of The Revolution had been cemented by a cameo in the film. Huntsberry has to take some share of the blame for Prince's weird public persona, having given the *National Enquirer* an interview that (as published) portrayed the boss as a paranoid wacko. Paisley Park contracts have ever since contained gagging clauses, applicable even after leaving Prince's employ.

The Moral Majority was quick to identify Prince as the latest threat to the nation's morals. Back home in St Paul a pair of evangelical brothers, Dan and Steve Peters, ultra-strict constructionists when it came to biblical provisions for music (basically, Psalms of David, angelic trumpets and choirs = good, everything else = bad), waged a campaign against the local boy, asking teenagers to help save the Twin Cities from turning into the Cities of the Plain by burning copies of *Dirty Mind* and *Purple Rain*. Interestingly, in 2004, the brothers no longer mention Prince on their website, instead promoting the evangelical songs of born-again Mark Farner (formerly of Grand Funk Railroad) and reserving their spleen for those *faux*-Christian acts that camouflage their commitment to the Devil's music with gospel choruses. For a time, though, he was their favourite whipping boy.

Prince was about to throw the cultural conservatives a more lasting hostage to fortune. One evening in 1984, the wife of senator Al Gore, who sixteen years later would win a presidential election but still not make it to the White House, overheard their daughter listening to *Purple Rain*. She was shocked by the lyrical content. It would be entertaining to report that Karenna Gore was so thoroughly corrupted by 'Darling Nikki' (apparently the offending track) that she threw in her lot with Prince, took to wearing flimsy basques and made a career as lead singer of Karenna 6. Disappointingly, she is now a very serious and ardent Democratic campaigner, a job which presumably rules out self-pleasuring in hotel lobbies. Her bedroom listening did, however, lead to Tipper Gore and Susan Baker, wife of the then Treasury Secretary James Baker, founding the Parents Music Resource Center which now provides the PARENTAL ADVISORY stickers intended to warn families of offensive content but now more often used by teenagers to determine whether there's anything really worth listening to on a rock or hip-hop album. Ironically, one of the first albums slated for such a sticker was the infamous *Black Album*, which was pulled before release.

The tabloid stories were a mixed blessing for Prince, part irritant, part short-term free publicity. In the longer perspective, the image they created of the star as an eccentric outsider, involved in just about every conceivable perversity up to but not including child molestation (that was a charge reserved for his biggest market rival in black pop-soul), alienated any sympathy Prince might have received during his later corporate tussles. For the moment at least, he was riding on a wave of intriguing headlines and still enjoying the indulgent patronage of the parent label.

* * *

Warner Brothers were indulgent enough to humour their star in a fresh and expensive game of charades. Having followed *Purple Rain* with a wonky new musical direction, Prince was again minded to dabble in film. Almost everything about *Under the Cherry Moon* is wrong. Without the fragile anchor of autobiography, the story creaks and the script lumbers. Prince's obsessive direction – he took over from first-timer Mary Herbert once the film was in production – gives a fine and largely British cast the air of a well-drilled am. dram. group. His own performance, as the piano-playing gigolo Christopher Tracy, isn't so much wooden as plastic. Again, the one redeeming feature is a lively soundtrack. Released in March 1986, not as an OST, but as if it were a freestanding album ('Music from the motion picture . . .' is relegated to the small print), *Parade* still suffered from its association with a film that barely cleared $3 million in its opening week, a first taste of public failure. It did, however, yield another classic single, perhaps the last in Prince's career to deliver the paradigm-shifting slap of a 'When Doves Cry' or a 'Purple Rain'.

Filmed on the French Riviera and originally in colour, later reprocessed to black and white in accordance with Prince's wishes, the movie acts out a strange social and ethnic ritual which is interesting enough to counterbalance its obvious dramatic insufficiencies. The basic premise is that heiress Mary Sharon (played by the glacial Kristin Scott Thomas) stands to claim the trust fund set up by her father (Steven Berkoff, visibly contemplating how he's going to spend his fee), but only when she marries. Christopher decides he's the man for the job and dedicates himself to taking some of the white middle-class starch out of her.

The monochrome release actually sharpens the story's racial subtext; to that extent at least Prince's directorial instincts were spot on. In shaping his character (actually not much more than a series of still portraits animated by attitude) Prince seems to have returned to the mixed-blood glamour he projected in rawer form on *Dirty Mind*. It's one of the few occasions where he deliberately uses street language and argot as a signifier. He even debates the possibility of 'passing' for white with his friend Tricky (Family member Jerome Benton in a role that seems tailor-made for the estranged Morris Day), though their dramatic function seems to be mischief rather than assimilation: two sharp young blacks bent on putting a bit of sexual and musical oomph into strait-laced and unfunky whites, as they do when they clear a smart restaurant with the joyous funk of 'Girls & Boys'. What to make, then, of the climax, when Berkoff, outraged that his daughter has fallen in love with this archetypally protean Trickster, guns him down? Is miscegenation such a potent taboo, or are we merely being spared the complication of a married (and wealthy) hero and the dismal sight of him succumbing to stiff-backed domesticity?

If *Under the Cherry Moon* is clunky as social anthropology, its historical underpinnings creak alarmingly. Ostensibly set in 1930s France, where its black and half-caste exoticism has a certain authenticity, the film is unmistakably 1980s in its emphases and, for all the dressing-up, hasn't left Uptown and Paisley Park. The anachronism is perhaps more clever than first appears. The film's nostalgic overtones both disguise and point up the avant-gardism of the music. Prince also seems to be exploring an older, certainly pre-1960s construction of black identity, projecting himself as a jive-talking outsider who is nonetheless so fascinated by white society that he seems to identify with it. There have been many mixed-race entertainers in American popular culture, but the default position has always been that if they possess even a quarter element of non-Caucasian blood, they are defined as black. What Prince did was to create, for the first time, a genuine biracialism. It's one of the central axes of his imagination, and alongside it his own personal version of the Saturday night/Sunday morning dichotomy. What makes it personal is that Prince eroticises spirituality rather than using it as a redeeming contrast.

* * *

The commercial failure of *Under the Cherry Moon* and that film's obvious fantasy structure and period setting prob- ably meant that fans and reviewers were less inclined to mine *Parade* for autobiographical references. Perversely, though, it also led to a certain musical inattention. Though individually, and with one obvious exception, the album's tracks are less striking than those on *1999*, *Purple Rain* and even the maverick *Around the World in a Day*, *Parade* is arguably his most sophisticated work structurally.

The most immediately obvious musical difference that separates *Parade* from its predecessors is that Prince seems to have overcome his dislike of horns. There are hints of classic swing right from the start, presumably the influence of John Nelson, who co-wrote 'Christopher Tracy's Parade' and 'Under the Cherry Moon'. Saxophonist Eric Leeds is strongly featured on 'Girls & Boys' and along with trumpeter Atlanta Bliss (originally Matt Blistan) became a member of the touring band, giving The Revolution a tighter funk sound, less dependent on synths and distorted guitar. Prince also uses strings on the album for the first time (beautifully arranged by Clare Fischer, who had worked on The Family's album), while the brass and woodwind rosters reveal some highly marketable jazz names: trombonists Garnett Brown and Bill Watrous, trumpeter Ray Brown and reed specialists Gary Foster and Jack Nimitz. Unusually, Prince uses another rhythm guitarist, the enigmatically named Mico (actually Miko Weaver), on 'Mountains'. Percussion is added here and there by Sheila E and Jonathan Melvoin.

The other voices include his sisters Wendy and Susannah (picture Prince's delight at having white twins on his record and in his videos), Lisa and Sheila on 'Girls & Boys', which also features a spoken 'French seduction' by Marie France. A solitary backing vocal from protégé Mazarati on 'Kiss' and 'a little gypsy girl', actually Sandra Francisco, on 'Do You Lie?'. He's still very much in control of the music, but Prince increasingly wants to differentiate character and to explore different shades of vocal colour. His own falsetto is less in evidence and there is more of a Billy Eckstine croon to his voice, again a period touch.

That said, the album's strongest track is very much a reworking of the formula that made 'When Doves Cry' such an iconic track. For a start, Prince reverts to falsetto but like the earlier track 'Kiss' has no bassline and hangs on a single devastating rhythm guitar track. Apparently, there was a fuller version put together with the members of Mazarati (a side project of Mark Brown's), but in one of his brilliantly minimalist coups Prince dismantled it. Cleverly again, on the video Prince consigns the guitar part to Wendy Melvoin. In fact, she takes the male role. She 'plays', mugs, winces and flirts indulgently as he dances with a semi-naked partner draped in black; in a clever sight gag, the anonymous dancer mouths the only deep-voiced sound. The whole thing is ironically framed by a TV set. It's a great song, joyous, attractively lewd and for all its stop–start quality, utterly danceable and undimmed by Tom Jones's later cover version.

Ever the master of exclusion, Prince leaves off the percussion on 'Sometimes It Snows in April', the melancholy ballad which ends the album and finally explains that enigmatic remark to Steve Fargnoli. It's constructed around piano and acoustic guitar. 'Venus de Milo' is another piano track. 'Mountains' is a bit of mystical nonsense that might have sat just as well on *Around the World in a Day*. 'Life Can Be So Nice' is another homage to The Beatles, albeit in their darker and more ironic incarnation. 'Anotherloverholenyohead' is brilliant, brittle confessional pop. Much of this sandwiched between the fanfare opening that immediately precedes 'Christopher Tracy's Parade' and 'End', which frames the original LP A-side.

Parade only yielded one stone classic in 'Kiss' (though 'Anotherloverholenyohead', 'Girls & Boys' and 'Mountains' were all modestly successful singles), but it is a masterpiece in terms of album construction and a sign of his growing confidence in looking beyond the singles charts. If the movie served no other purpose than to provide a loose narrative structure, mood and sense of place for the record, then it succeeded. Unlike *Purple Rain*, where film and album were mutually reinforcing, Prince seemed inclined to play down the connectedness in the case of *Parade*. The cover art – a monochrome Prince in tiny black crop top over a crucifix and in dancer's pose – recalls the stark setting of the 'Kiss' video; *it* was to be the album's most successful supporting visual. Prince had at last learned to dance convincingly and to load his videos with playful references to the group. Parts assigned to the 'wrong' player have become a promo cliché (REM were represented by four Japanese non-lookalikes for the video of 'Crush with Eyeliner', a song which might just be Michael Stipe's half-conscious homage to Prince), but the play of black and white, twinned personalities and actual twins – an equally playful ambiguity as to whether the whole enterprise is dead serious or a put-on or both – is part of the subtlety that surrounds *Parade*. As a compilation of songs – and Prince at the time claimed to have more than 250 lying in his studio – it is in no way exceptional. As an album, though, it has for all its bewildering diversity an extraordinary coherence. The only expected element missing from *Parade* is a hint of the mystical transcendence, the overt spirituality, that runs through earlier and later records like a vein of quartz; missing, that is, unless one interprets 'Mountains' as a metaphor along the lines of the ladder on *Around the World in a Day*, and the video does point to that interpretation.

It is almost as if Prince has put aside his troublesome Christ-complex to cast himself as the Saved Thief who shared Calvary. The significance of 'Christopher' as a character name shouldn't be overlooked. As ever, the musical larceny is hooded and respectful: Lennon and McCartney in the structure and sequencing every bit as much as in some of the songs; old movie soundtracks; raw r'n'b – 'Kiss' takes him back to that night with Hayward Baker at a James Brown gig and the inevitable moment where everything dropped out except a screaming voice and an electric guitar; the record also has a looser, almost jazzy feel that might well reflect John Nelson's continuing influence. It's all there and more. *Parade* may be not just Prince's most overlooked record, but one of the unsung masterpieces of pop.

10

At the start of 1987, Prince had one more classic record left in him, quite possibly the greatest and most complex of all. If the story ended with the release of *Sign 'O' The Times*, his place with the angels would still be guaranteed. In the event, he was to make another fifteen records between then and 2004's mild, muted *Musicology* and 2006's rather better *3121*. Ask all but a devoted Prince fan to list them in chronological order and you'll get at best a hesitant reply. The next period of Prince's life was devoted largely to the development of his Paisley Park studio complex at Chanhassen outside Minneapolis, but within a few years he would fall out – terminally – with Warner Brothers, and lose his name. Some would say his mind went with it.

The consensus is that, after 1987, Prince also lost his audience. The truth is slightly more complex. If *Parade* saw Prince playfully exploring a new – albeit retro – definition of black identity, the next album marked a further but more measured retreat from the 'biracial' style that had won him millions of fans with *Purple Rain*. If Prince were Miles Davis, *Sign 'O' The Times* would be his *On the Corner*, on which the trumpeter deliberately aligned himself with a new constituency – hip, black, street-smart – and used his cover art to throw out an aggressively separatist gesture to the white fans whose loyalty was based entirely on Miles's willingness to recycle the same cool idiom.

Prince had failed to deliver *Purple Rain Mk II*, though perhaps by happy accident rather than shrewd strategic planning. His next two records, and the notorious 'bootleg' which became the most famous unreleased record since the Beach Boys' *SMiLE*, saw him turn back towards his original constituency. Both musically and in presentation, *Sign 'O' The Times* is a whiter album than *Parade* but the continuing slide in sales – it peaked at number six in the *Billboard* chart (its predecessor made it to number three) – was a sign that the notoriously fickle white audience was drifting away from a musician who seemed addicted to unpredictability. Either that, or he was drifting away from them.

Even so, *Sign 'O' The Times*' cover is a muted version of *Purple Rain*'s raw cityscape – a montage of a faked-up neon background over a yellow-toned and flower-strewn stage set. Sheila E's drum riser is a large car with busted, painted-over lights and Minnesota plates. Prince's phallic yellow guitar lies abandoned just below it. The words 'Paradise Set', rather than the title of the album, are written at the bottom, but it seems to be if not Paradise Lost then certainly Paradise Abandoned. There is no sign of The Revolution either in person or on the cover credit, and Prince himself, wearing eyeglasses and looking wary, is out-of-focus and disappearing out of frame at bottom right as if he's walking away not just from the disbanded Revolution but from the multiple pleasures promised in the retro neon backdrop. On stage and on camera, Prince has always cultivated a devastating ability to single you out with a look; it's disconcerting for once *not* to meet his eye and read his intentions.

Can his mind be on things other than himself, you, and the possibility of seduction? There is a teasing clue right there in the title, where the 'O' is actually a nuclear disarmament sign (in the US usually described as a peace sign); and there is a striking new tone to the title track which opens the album on a long, weary-voiced litany of the world's ills. Added to the familiar liberal roster – guns, crime, war, drugs, poverty – is the virus that in the mid-1980s wriggled into Prince's sexual Eden and rendered his brand of unfettered desire steadily more unfashionable as the decade ran on. Given what follows on the record, it's premature to label *Sign 'O' The Times* as Prince's *What's Going On?* or Prince as a freshly 'engaged' or even mildly 'concerned' artist.

When Live Aid happened in 1984, the only stars to crack the mood of weirdly jubilant anxiety about the planet's wrongs were both from Minnesota. Bob Dylan's *faux pas* was to suggest that some of the proceeds should be directed to America's farmers rather than to Africa; Prince's was not

to turn up at all. Later he did contribute a track – the so-
so '4 the Tears in Your Eyes' – for the *USA For Africa* album.
His decision three years later to graft a social comment song
into *Sign 'O' The Times*, indeed to place it first on the album,
wasn't so much missionary zeal as a brilliantly wrong-footing
tactic that highlights the record's dominant mood of erotic
subtlety and softens the listener up (if that's the right expression) for the chastened optimism of 'The Cross'.

Nowhere else in his work has Prince so carefully blended
his spectrum of musical styles. James Brown funk sits
alongside Joni Mitchell imagism, gospel, punk and anthem
rock, all co-existing in a richly improvisatory collage.

* * *

If Prince came of age as an engineer with *1999*, by the time
he released *Sign 'O' The Times* he was in the process of
creating his very own state-of-the-art engineering set-up.
The Paisley Park studio complex is located about half an
hour's drive to the west of Minneapolis centre at 7801
Audubon Parkway in the dormitory suburb of Chanhassen.
The $10-million complex, designed by Prince himself and
looking very much that way, is pictured on the inside
booklet of *Emancipation* with a weird-looking Prince posed
in front of his white BMW. The studios were officially
opened on September 11, 1987, but parts of *Sign* were
recorded there, as well as at the familiar Sunset Sound. The
new set-up featured two forty-eight-track recording studios

as well as a 12,000-square-foot soundstage where Prince and anyone else who cared to book the facility (takers have included Barry Manilow, The Bee Gees, George Benson, Steve Miller and even, improbably, REM) can rehearse stage shows, shoot videos and even put on full-scale concerts. Like the mansion at Lake Minnetonka, it was widely seen as another *folie de grandeur*, but it provided Prince with a working space and power base that seemed to strengthen his creative independence.

It also provided fans with an instant shrine, a Graceland minus the tombstone but featuring the latest technology. Tours became an obligatory station on a Twin Cities pilgrimage, and a rival attraction to Bob McCoy's celebrated Museum of Questionable Sexual Devices, always with the faint lure of a personal appearance by the Questionable Sexual Practitioner himself. Such manifestations were rare, though Prince was still occasionally spotted in Minneapolis clubs, checking out the talent, seemingly happy in the role of local boy made good. What the tours did serve was to dent the notion of the artist as a reclusive paranoiac, hiding inside what might have passed as a supervillain's lair in a Bond movie.

If Paisley Park was Prince's Xanadu, its fortunes ebbed and flowed with his. His decision to keep it open – and therefore manned – 24/7, just in case the recording muse struck in the middle of the night, as it was apt to do, contributed substantially to Prince's financial problems of the mid-1990s. By then, there were outstanding bills, and

Prince's step-brother Duane – not the most reliable operative on the planet – was in nominal charge, following the departure of Paisley Park Enterprises president Gilbert Davison. The studios were effectively closed between 1996, the nadir of Prince's personal, commercial and critical arc, and the summer of 2004, when they reopened newly digitalised and upgraded. Listening to *Sign 'O' The Times* is a little like running your hand over the brand new headquarters' dust-free surfaces and wiggling your toes in the plush carpets reserved for its private areas. It is Prince's most sensuous – as opposed to sensual – record, a hymn to increasingly responsible pleasures. It also dramatises perfectly his ongoing effort to meld sin and redemption, thoughtful engagement and thoughtless indulgence, and to show off stolen wares with the confidence of ownership. The Thief had his own temple at last.

* * *

The opening is, again, a surprise. A marimba-like figure and expectant drumbeats are punctuated by the kind of erotic yelp – 'Oh, yeah' – that suggests funky, James Brown soul. Then, the single most astonishing opening in the entire Prince canon. 'In France a skinny man died of a big disease with a little name . . .'; his girlfriend picks up a needle and goes the same way; a gang of seventeen-year-olds called The Disciples (!) do crack and pack machine-guns; a black girl kills her baby because she can't afford to feed it; in

September 'my cousin' tries hash for the first time and by June he's doing heroin – all followed by the devastating, sarcastic hook, they're 'silly', these signs o' the times.

What's often overlooked is that interwoven with these relatively generic ills are references to the *Challenger* disaster (which happened on January 28, 1986) and to the moment when a church roof is ripped off by 'Hurricane Annie' (a half-conscious echo of the time when 'Annie Christian' was the repository of all that was wrong with the world). These are more subtle reminders of human hubris, but possibly also of hope, because after the space shuttle explosion everyone still wanted to fly.

The clinching astonishment is the song's conclusion. After repeating the old, fatalistic assertion that no one's really happy until they're dead, Prince exhorts us to hurry up before it's too late, but not to join him in the apocalyptic orgy of *1999*: 'Let's fall in love, get married, have a baby / We'll call him Nate (if it's a boy).' It's a 'silly' pay-off, but love, marriage, babies? This can't be *Prince*, surely, even if he is being ironic?

In 1987, time, as well as 'the times', was beginning to weigh more heavily on him. His thirtieth birthday was just a year away. There is a strong sense of haste around *Sign 'O' The Times*, which comes out of the busiest year of Prince's entire career. *Sign 'O' The Times* is a double album, his first since *1999*. Unlike the baggy monsters of later years, every track justifies its place. If there really were hundreds of songs lying in his studio, he was determined to get them down on tape, not just because Paisley Park meant he could do, but also because he had to. It is the classic nihilist's dilemma: what to do when the apocalypse fails to happen?

Even after the gentle pay-off to the title-track, we're still prepared for something darker and more sober from the rest. The next song begins with another ecstatic soul wail – 'Ooh doggies' – and the sound of an ambulance dopplering past but 'Play in the Sunshine' is all danceable, piano-driven pop, with just the minor proviso that the promised pleasure is taken without the help of 'a Margarita or Exstacy [sic]'. It's a curious track, rendered less transparent from following the title song, but also because the fiery guitar solo at its heart sits oddly with the nursery rhyme lyrics, stuff about four-leafed clovers, 'pop goes the music' and a big, white, talking rabbit. Dancing 'like it's gonna be the last time' is another throwback reference, but again instead of mindless partying we're asked to love our enemies until the 'gorilla' – initially misheard as 'mirror' – 'falls off the wall'. Is this the young black-and-white movie freak remembering that epic of failed love and bigotry *King Kong*, or is it something altogether simpler?

Natural disaster is recast as celebration on 'Housequake', the B-side of 'U Got the Look' and a disco favourite. Here is a falsetto Prince as *alter ego* 'Camille', with vocal party favours from engineers Susan Rogers, Coke Johnson and others. Punctuated by a camply petulant 'Shut up already, damn!', the shouty vocal has a cheerfully retro 'dance craze' feel, even namechecking the Twist. Prince yelps. Eric

Leeds and Atlanta Bliss blare their horns like members of the JBs.

In contrast to the title track and the truly bizarre song which follows, 'Housequake' is content-free. 'The Ballad of Dorothy Parker' is one of Prince's strangest creations. Dorothy is a dishwater blonde waitress on the promenade, with a sharp tongue (so it may be a nickname). Prince's character has been 'talking stuff / In a violent room / Fighting with lovers past'. He goes to the restaurant and, not very hungry, orders a fruit cocktail. She makes a sarcastic comment about his manhood, but finds him cute and suggests he takes a bath. He insists on keeping his pants on. She puts on the radio and listen to her favourite song, Joni Mitchell's 'Help Me', from Prince's and the Melvoins' favourite *Court and Spark* album. (Joni certainly knows of the literary Dorothy Parker, even if it's hard to imagine Prince being a fan.) The phone rings. Dorothy says whoever it is can't be as cute as him. The pants come off, but Dorothy hasn't read the script. 'Instead she pretended she was blind / An affliction brought on by a witch's curse.' Prince goes back to his violent room but next time the fighting starts he takes another bubble bath with his pants on, and that makes everything right.

There are a few obvious interpretations. Is this a screened memory of a real-life encounter, perhaps when the teenage Prince was out on the streets, midway between John Nelson's and Bernadette Anderson's? Did some kindly, brassy dame take pity on the kid and offer him a bath? Like his memory of that dancer outside his father's club, it smells of fantasy sprinkled over a more neutral encounter. The mention of violence is the one thing that makes it troubling. Prince says he dreamed the whole thing, which only half-answers the question. It's an odd-sounding track, very bottomy and almost submarine, perhaps because it was recorded at the yet to be opened Paisley Park on a half-built desk.

Again, Prince sequences the album brilliantly. Like the later 'Hot Thing', 'IT' is pure lustful funk, though you're still left wondering whether this is the same damaged kid in the diner who's singing. 'Starfish and Coffee' is a delightful schooldays fantasy, with a hook – '. . . Maple syrup and jam / Butterscotch clouds, a tangerine / And a side order of ham' – as infectious as the 'flu. Originally intended for the abandoned *Dream Factory* album, it was co-written with Susannah, and further evidence of the Melvoins' devotion to Joni Mitchell and The Beatles; there's even a 'Lucy' in there along with Kevin, Miss Kathleen and the far from ordinary Cynthia Rose, whose breakfast menu provides that mad chorus. Next up is 'Slow Love', swathed in Claire Fischer's strings, while 'Forever in My Life' ends the first disc with a promise of unfailing fidelity. It's a song he has reworked more than almost any other.

By now, the listener has been well primed to expect the unexpected, but why assign the male lead vocal of 'U Got the Look', which opens the second disc, to 'Camille', when it's billed as 'Boy versus Girl in the World Series of Love'. What complicates the picture still more is that it's the girl who's playing tough as a whole new racial scenario is played out, coloured peach and black. (It's often forgotten that yellow and peach are also signature Prince hues.) Sheila E provides limber jazz percussion, but it's Sheena E who acts out the other half of this curious number, which again finds Prince using a self-consciously black argot – 'U sho'nuf be cookin' in my book' – as (s)he goes about a notably rough and ready wooing. The key rhyme – '. . . jammin' . . . heck-a-slammin' / If love is good, let's get 2 rammin'' – doesn't suggest the same Prince as sides one and two with their promise of 'Slow Love' and undying affection.

At first glance 'If I Was Your Girlfriend' sounds like another attempt to cast himself in a female role, but it's more subtle than that. This is Prince, again tricked out as Camille, wondering wistfully, even weepily, how things might be different between men and women if they could only make like good girlfriends instead of lovers. So subtle are the sexual politics here that we're creeping perilously close to post-post-feminism. Why won't she undress in front of 'him'? Why can't 'he' help without making her feel helpless? The break in that small voice when he goes 'Plea-hea-hease' is heartbreaking and funny by turns; it's as if James Brown's kid sister got up on stage to do 'Please, Please, Please'. But then Camille drops into a husky speaking voice, thick with desire as she lists all the things she'd like to do, including kissing you 'down there, where it really counts', promising to drink up 'every ounce'. There is hardly a better, franker, more emotionally honest love song in the whole history of pop and soul and what makes it musically is that where you'd expect to hear Lisa, Wendy and Susannah touching in the background harmonies, it's a chorus of gruff-voiced 'men', murmuring their assent.

After that, 'Strange Relationship' is an anticlimax, though the accompaniment of sitar and wooden flute (Lisa) is reminiscent of *Around the World in a Day*, not least in that the instrumental component is no longer locked tight, but loose and almost improvisational in feel. Even 'I Could Never Take the Place of Your Man', a country song *manqué* and in every way a Prince solo effort, has a relaxed and unhurried air. It's another song about sex versus long-term commitment, addressed to a girl who's been abandoned with a baby and another on the way. The singer concedes he's qualified for a one-night stand, but . . . cue title. Lustful but mature and self-denying; how to have your cake and eat it.

It would make some sense for *Sign 'O' The Times* to end with 'The Cross'. It makes a perfect bookend with the title track, except this time redemption is promised: 'He is coming'. It's a slow-building song built over a simple, almost Eastern guitar line reminiscent of a welter of 1960s rock from The Byrds to Grateful Dead and The Doors. The Fugees' hip-hop version, which delighted the composer, preserves that mysterioso feel. The initial mood is stormy, but the ghettos to the left are balanced by flowers to the right and by the promise of bread for all, 'If we can just bear the Cross'. After monumental drum beats, a heavier guitar riff starts to cut across, rising to a crescendo reminiscent of 'Purple Rain''s. Here, though, the salvation is explicitly Christian and not erotic.

It's one of Prince's finest rock performances and was an electrifying spectacle on tour where it was done in clerical garb. The album isn't quite over, though. Almost anything else would be bathos, but 'It's Gonna Be a Beautiful Night', recorded in front of '6,000 beautiful Parisians' on the French leg of the last Revolution tour, is a brilliant encore, uniting the whole augmented line-up (it was co-written with Dr Fink and Eric Leeds) for one last hurrah. That, too, would mark a satisfying full stop, but Prince follows it with one last song. 'Adore' is a more earthly expression of love, albeit expressed in a gospelly sway that underpins the final, unambiguous benediction: '4 all time I am with U / U are with me.'

* * *

He'd never before made an album that touched on so many musical styles and moods so effectively. At every point, generic expectations are cranked up and then deftly subverted. Prince detourns the popular song, not just by playing his usual thematic games but by radically expanding what is possible in a popular song. Some over-emphasis on the lyrics is essential, because the music is so hard to 'read', full of mysterious dissonance and deceptively lightweight melodic ideas. Like the symbol he was shortly to become in place of a name, *Sign 'O' The Times* 'doesn't pronounce; it just *is*'.

It might just have been even bigger had Prince been allowed to release the three-LP set – apparently to be known as *Crystal Ball* – which he'd originally envisaged. Triple albums had a bad reputation, suggesting the worst excesses of prog rock, and Warner refused to countenance this one, the beginnings perhaps of what was soon to become an unbridgeable divide between the label and its most mercurial artist. He only got his way almost a decade later with the odd and overblown, but still intriguing *Emancipation*.

Sign 'O' The Times does point a way forward, even if it wasn't quite the broad yellow highway Prince envisaged. Whereas in the past he had made records which condensed much of his listening experience, his sense of a musical past, *Sign 'O' The Times* represents a commitment to a musical future. Its strangely unfinished feel and lack of obvious hits was, as Michelangelo Matos senses in his tiny, very personal monograph on the album, part of a commitment to a new phase of activity in which history played less of a part.

The opening of Paisley Park had given Prince unprecedented creative freedom, more even than Warner's indulgent contract (which now included an autonomous label imprint), more even than the runaway commercial success of *Purple Rain*. With a studio and soundstage available to him, the flow of recorded material seemed staunchless; leftover material from *Sign 'O' The Times* eventually appeared on *Graffiti Bridge*. A further album was slated for release in December. In the event, it only made an official appearance seven years later, and then for a limited period. By 1994, though, almost everyone who wanted to hear *The Black Album* owned the bootleg vinyl or a C90 copy; almost everyone else had heard *of* it and knew it to be the journeywork of the Devil, packed with unspeakable sexual references and diabolic invocations. Few records have gained so much in stature from *not* being released. But *The Black Album* had missed its historical moment and when it was officially released it seemed like nothing more than a basic funk album, horny but ordinary.

Almost as soon as it was withdrawn, rumours began to circulate that the album was far more extreme, far more sexually graphic than anything Prince had previously attempted. It was even suggested that its increasingly mature and responsible creator was shocked by what had erupted from his own unconscious. (He put a secret message into the video for 'Alphabet St', the hit single from *Lovesexy*, that read 'Don't buy *The Black Album*. I'm sorry.') More convincing than self-censorship was the possibility that Prince was unwilling to see his work issued with one of the new PARENTAL ADVISORY stickers. Others said that he was merely dissatisfied with the work and that *The Black Album* was being stripped down to its components to create a fresh mix. Some claimed, on no solid evidence, that it was actually so bad as to be unrescuable. Engineer Susan Rogers has hinted that it was never intended for commercial release in the first place, and that it was no more than a collection of oddments only put on vinyl to be deejayed at a party for Sheila E. An imaginatively paranoid spin on events suggested that Warner actually regarded the bootleg culture that had grown up around Prince – such as the *Camille* cassettes – as useful back-channel promotion, cheaper than a full-scale ad campaign, and actually encouraged 'suppression' of the record. Prince told *USA Today* that he'd been inspired to replace the record with *Lovesexy* after seeing the name of God spelt out in clouds over a field . . .

The Truth is almost inevitably more banal, but with enough of Prince's capricious streak in play to make a story of it. Given that he had already released a double album in 1987, and that sales for *Sign 'O' The Times* were relatively slow, it would have been commercial folly to release another disc in December and dent the earlier record's chances of making up some ground in the Christmas market. Why, once the decision had been taken, Prince didn't simply bump *The Black Album* down the issue schedule a matter of months isn't clear. Whatever the reason, it acquired an instant mystique; leaked original vinyl copies are alleged to have changed hands for more than $10,000.

* * *

The danger of pumped-up reputations – and black market prices – is that the debunking and the market devaluation usually go too far. Having billed *The Black Album* as the biggest, baddest, horniest yet, the media were all too quick to write it off as a soft-centred flop. Mainstream reviewers, though, only had a chance to review the album when it made a brief official appearance between late November 1994 and late January 1995, seven years after it was recorded. By then, the music industry had seen grunge come and go, and gangsta rap come and stay, and behind them a steady throb of sexually graphic r'n'b inspired by Prince but often maturely confident enough to bypass his adolescent flagrancy. What parents' groups charmingly refer to as four-, seven-, twelve- and thirteen-letter words were no longer a novelty in popular music.

Prince's creative decline is significantly counterbalanced, possibly even outweighed, by his remarkable consistency and prolific longevity. As Stuart Cosgrove shrewdly pointed out in the *NME*, he was the antithesis of the self-destructive rock star, a controlled and controlling figure who could no more have stopped producing music than he could have put a shotgun in his mouth, plummeted into drug abuse, or driven around looking for rivals with an Uzi in the back of his white T-Bird. A further, unexpected factor in his seeming drift was the steady disintegration of Michael Jackson. Two masters of self-transformation, but only one of them wise enough to go down a non-surgical route. Where Prince played at being a pervert, Jackson ended up in court. While Michael tried to develop an androgynous persona by mimicking Elizabeth Taylor and Diana Ross, Prince invented Camille and then put her back in the box. He also found a way of sublimating his creative femininity into work for other artists and letting his own work flow unstaunched, without the painstaking obsession that restricted his rival to an album every three or four years.

Unlike Jackson, Prince has confronted the most difficult creative dilemma there is in popular music, that of growing old. For all the over-publicised traumas, tantrums and oddities of the 1990s, he has done so with remarkable authority and self-possession, the ludicrous cover of 1988's *Lovesexy* notwithstanding. *Sign 'O' The Times* was the first earnest expression of a desire to mature artistically without betraying his most basic energies. *The Black Album*'s curious history and curious, displaced position in the Prince discography is the sharpest reminder of how treacherous a concept artistic 'development' can be. Its initial shadowy status warped critical expectations; its eventual appearance made it seem, perversely, like a backward step rather than a defiant response to the criticism that with *Sign 'O' The Times* he had moved too far in the direction of mainstream pop. That is, by whatever measure, an absurd criticism. The record sustains a free-flowing, almost improvisatory style over four sides, a quality that was even more evident when he toured the record and changed songs, often quite radically, night after night. The habit of playing club dates straight after rock shows had become standard practice on the *Parade* tour, perhaps because the music there had been got down too tight. With *Sign 'O' The Times* Prince perhaps needed less of that jazzier outlet.

The challenge was to show that he could still make a record in the mould of *Dirty Mind*, but invest it with something new. He also needed to show that he could function at all levels without The Revolution. The band was disbanded before *Sign 'O' The Times* and isn't credited, though band members appear on various tracks. At the final show, in Yokohama Stadium, he'd done something unprecedented and smashed all the guitars on stage; just as Keith Richards had a different guitar for every number, Prince liked to say he had one for every emotion, except presumably nostalgia. He'd probably seen Richards' line-up on the ill-fated Stones tour, and he wasn't going to be allowed to forget the connection, when some critics suggested that the double album *Sign 'O' The Times* was his *Exile on Main Street*.

Prince's productivity had never been greater – he'd also written all the material for new Paisley Park signings Madhouse, a part-time fusion band featuring Eric Leeds and others – but *The Black Album* was again very much a solo project, without the collaborative energy he'd drawn from the band; drawn, and perhaps drained. Prince has an uncanny ability to take what he needs from a situation, introject it, and then move on. It can look callous, but it more often comes from creative imperatives than a lack of personal loyalty. His image as a man whose only friends are employees is misleading, but hard to argue against. Some thought there were circumstantial parallels between *The Black Album* and idol Sly Stone's *There's a Riot Going On*, which was also made at a moment of isolation, or, as Gavin Martin put it in a January 1988 issue of *New Musical Express* (even a Prince bootleg got the full review treatment), the record was a 'definitive example of a star's support system caving in around him as he came to terms with the outside world'. Martin's implication was that *Riot* was a masterpiece, and *The Black Album* was not.

* * *

It isn't a great album, but it's more than good. There's an air of haste, a lack of finish to the whole package, but it contains some of the best and most adventurous songs Prince had made in his whole first decade. Originally to be called *The Funk Bible*, it was a bid for a more stripped-down, blacker sound than the looser, rock-tinged work of recent years. It doesn't always come up to snuff. 'Cindy C' is a dull 'love song' to model and MTV jockette Cindy Crawford. 'Bob George', though, is hysterical, not least for its growling reference (a slowed-down vocal) to 'that skinny little motherfucker Prince'. It is one of his cleverest satirical personae, a cartoon gangster snarling at girlfriend Cathy Glover – known on tour as dancer Cat, and the object of some of Prince's most blatant onstage antics – for hanging out with rock'n'roll types. Much of the record, though, is pure dance material. The opening 'Le Grind' (with Sheila E, Cat and new recruit Boni Boyer on backing vocals) is a delight; sexy and smart. 'Supercalifragifunkysexy' is pure P-Funk and an anticipation of later dealings with George Clinton, while 'Rock Hard in a Funky Place' is as hard as Prince gets. '2 Nigs United 4 West Compton' is a fine instrumental that mixes and mangles stylistic elements with almost insulting ease. It also contains a reference to the growing boom in rap and hip-hop, something he comes back to in 'Dead on It'. It's often said that this is where Prince shows he's backed the wrong horse by dismissing all rappers as tone deaf. Listen carefully, though, and it's clear that he means the New York posse only, fit only to be cut to ribbons by the new Minneapolis crew. The only real ballad on the album, 'When 2 R in Love' would eventually appear on *Lovesexy*.

Before it was withdrawn, *The Black Album* had appeared in the Warner Brothers release schedule as by 'Somebody'. Whether its title was a further attempt at anonymity, an affirmation of colour, or a reference to a famous Beatles bootleg (and by extension to the so-called *White Album*) is open to speculation. Whatever the case, it enhanced the record's curious glamour. Ironically, it was Prince's next album that was to be subject to market censorship.

11

Lovesexy was Prince's tenth release in ten years. Some – even the most ardent fans – mark 1988 as the year when the wheels came off the wagon, yet his powers were still undimmed; in purely structural terms, *Lovesexy* was the most ambitious album to date, part of an ongoing cycle of experiment triggered by the deliberate backlash of *Around the World in a Day*, the avant-garde funk of *Parade* and the gradual disappearance of rock from his sound. The only forceful evidence that there might be something amiss at Paisley Park or rather in the ever more securely defended place that was Prince's head was the way he chose to appear on the cover. Wal-Mart's buyers took a look at it and decided this was one album they wouldn't be stocking.

If there really is a meaningful distinction between the nude and the merely naked – as art historians insist – Prince collapses it. If Jeff Koons were ever commissioned to design a production of *A Midsummer Night's Dream*, this is how he might imagine Puck, part forest spirit, part bum-boy, and whether human-scale or elfin depends on how you view the perspective. Prince reclines on the petals of a giant flower, surrounded by lilies, one of which turns a phallic purple stamen towards his pouting mouth. The left leg is raised to conceal his groin. The expression is remote, the sort of gaze one sees in eroticised images of martyrdom. The right hand rests on his heart, hiding what is presumably a crucifix, perhaps covering one of St Sebastian's wounds. The narrow beard and moustache are male, but the legs are elegant, clean-shaven, feminine; the hair is swept back to reveal a widow's peak that gives the whole ensemble a strangely Mephistophelian air.

The title track features an extraordinary moment where Cat's voice speeds up in an orgasmic chatter only to morph into Prince's as it slows down again. Elsewhere, he portrays himself as surrounded by women – they're constantly audible in the background – but they behave more like sexy choristers at the Rev. Al Green's church than a bunch of funky girlfriends. *Lovesexy* is Prince's most thoroughly spiritual album, packed with references to the power of love and sex to bring us closer to God; but it is also his most Manichean statement, portraying a world in which love, embodied by *Lovesexy*, faces the physical and metaphysical challenge of Spooky Electric. This mysterious adversary appears in the album's opening and closing tracks in a role somewhat similar to 'Annie Christian', but there are hints that Prince doesn't simply intend the usual unholy trinity of drugs, alcohol and violence, but something more subtly psychological. Spooky Electric feeds on our flaws, or as

Prince puts it, hang-ups, but only if we let him: 'Hold on 2 your soul / Don't kiss the beast'.

It's actually misleading to refer to 'tracks' on *Lovesexy* since the album is sequenced as a single continuous suite. It is the first Prince album conceived of and delivered as a CD, rather than as two – or four – vinyl sides, and the first to explore the new and by no means universal format. In retrospect, the other defining character of *Sign* is that it marks Prince's farewell to vinyl. Made in just seven weeks, *Lovesexy* was his attempt to sustain certain ideas – heaven/hell, nature/artifice, good/evil – and a carefully modulated mood over forty-five minutes. He did so by perversely introducing more new versions of himself than on any other record to date.

The other defining presence of the record is the Spirit Child, played by Minneapolis performance artist Ingrid Chavez, who turns up at the very start of ' No' to recite one of Prince's nursery rhyme funk lines in a dreamy voice: 'Rain is wet and sugar is sweet / Clap your hands and stamp your feet.' Prince then cuts in with a strangely sarcastic message – the reason his voice is so sweet is that there's no smack in it – delivered in the kind of tone you might use to endorse shampoo. What follows is an orthodox 'Just say no' anti-drugs riff, but delivered in Prince's funky preacher mode to a strange accompaniment of party noises and found sounds.

It also provides him with a platform to announce the coming of 'the New Power Generation', here intended as a concept – the incarnation of New Power Soul – but soon to be the name of his third successful band. On *Lovesexy* Prince uses essentially the group that had launched *Sign 'O' The Times* at First Avenue in March 1987 and had been seen around the world on a successful tour film. The longest serving member was now Dr Fink, but building up some mileage with Prince were Eric Leeds and Atlanta Bliss, Miko Weaver and Cat. Sheila E brought in two new recruits from her own band, Levi Seacer Jr on bass and Boni Boyer on organ and vocals. Seacer became an important collaborator, sharing writing and production credits on some of the non-Prince tracks for *Graffiti Bridge*. Boyer, who died suddenly in 1996, gave the album some of its rapt, churchy quality.

It's Cat, though, who's hauled to stage front to rap on 'Alphabet St', a slice of stripped-down r'n'b built round a jangling guitar line, drums and handclaps, somewhat in the mould of 'When Doves Cry' and 'Kiss', and an obvious choice for first single. It's also Cat who ends the song with a lascivious recitation of the alphabet, dwelling a trifle too long on 'F', missing out 'G' altogether and stopping with 'I . . . love you'. Prince had never before deployed so many of his voices – anything from falsetto to bass, but also including the unexpected AOR tones of 'Glam Slam' – and what becomes obvious as the album progresses is that this is his most intensely *aural* album to date, a rich matrix of pure sound that often makes no obvious musical sense, yet functions musically at a very high level. Those who dismissed the album on release as a set of very ordinary tunes pointlessly embellished with sound effects were right, but right for the wrong reasons.

Prince had once again managed to invest banality with gravitas and mystery. The curious abstractions of *Sign 'O' The Times* are realised here as futuristic pop-funk. Where earlier he had used non-musical sound as an alienation device – bips and bleeps, a telephone bell, the addition of needle hiss, which later became a CD-era retro cliché, the bizarre coughing fit which precedes the 'Raspberry Beret' video – on *Lovesexy* such sounds have become part of the music itself. It's no coincidence that the *Lovesexy* tour was the most elaborate he ever attempted; and the most expensive – Prince barely broke even on it.

His ability to create whole environments, even within the bounds of a single song, are tested on 'Anna Stesia', a slow, swooning hymn to the God of Love and to a state of mind somewhere between anaesthesia and ecstasy. It also contains a rare, explicit reference to Jesus, something Prince has usually avoided. 'Dance On' has a touch of Hendrix's 'Machine Gun' riff, but pitched way down low in the bass and down as a dance track rather than an anti-war song. It's Sheila E's finest moment with Prince, vivid, multi-layered drumming that weds Ringo's backbeat to Elvin Jones's polyrhythms. The song ends with a rap: 'We need a new power structure that breeds production instead of jacks who vandalise', a perfect example of how Prince is able to change registers in mid-line. He does the same thing at the end of 'Lovesexy' itself when Cat morphs into Prince as she orgasms. The song also includes a sung setting of the Spirit Child's opening recitation, showing how tightly woven an album this is: but who's the singer? A mature 'rock' voice, new to the Prince canon.

The segue into 'When 2 R in Love' is simple but devastating. On the surface, it's a formulaic love ballad, but it betrays its origins as a *Black Album* 'shocker' with lines like 'the thought of his tongue in the V of her love in his mind'. Worth deconstructing carefully, because one of the implicit messages of *Lovesexy* is that physical love may be wonderful, but metaphysical love may be an even greater high, imagined pleasures even more intense than real ones: 'When 2 R in love – their bodies shiver at the mere contemplation of penetration let alone the actual act.'

If *Dirty Mind* was all provocation and prurience, *Lovesexy* is brilliantly and beautifully sublimated in an ebb and flow of feeling. The soft keyboard figures and running water effects at the end of 'Positivity' close the circle and end the album on a note of quiet benediction and acceptance. It's also the end of a phase in Prince's music. Like Miles Davis again, he'd started out wrestling with a genre that didn't quite express his fundamental creative needs (in Miles's case, bebop), had sensed the cultural paradigm shift represented by rock, had come through a period of abstraction (Miles's was much more savage) in order to create a new kind of musical beauty that was neither hot nor cool, neither visceral nor intellectual, but all of these at once.

Had Prince Nelson never again entered a recording

studio, the records he made between 1978 and 1988 would still guarantee him a permanent seat at popular music's high table, even if he were guaranteed to abuse the privilege. In that decade, as documented in Per Nilsen's meticulous sessionography *Dancemusicsexromance*, he had written, recorded, arranged and/or produced more than 250 recorded tracks that saw official release, together with about half that number that walked out of studios, off mixing desks, or into Sony Pros at parties, gigs and rehearsals.

* * *

It was no surprise that Prince's next venture should be a new kind of collaborative project rather than another 'Prince album'. It was no surprise that it centred on a figure who touches on perverse 'Princely' qualities. It's also no surprise that even in character as *Batman* – the comic-book and TV icon who'd obsessed him in childhood – Prince should obsess about the themes which had underpinned his previous two records: past, future and afterlife.

It took director Tim Burton and star Jack Nicholson some time to persuade Prince that he should take on the soundtrack for Warner Brothers' movie version of DC Comics' this-worldly superhero. From the studio's point of view, it was a perfect association, with or without a suggested input from Michael Jackson, and a subtly covert way of bending its most wayward star to corporate will. It also diverted Prince from work on a new album – eventually

Graffiti Bridge – which Warner thought was premature. If Jackson's suggested contribution was shelved, so were some of Prince's initial ideas, produced as usual at white heat. A new 'Batman Theme' was turned down, as were a couple of songs that resurfaced later, notably 'Rave Un2 the Joy Fantastic'. In the event, Danny Elfman provided an instrumental score for the film, while Prince created a body of songs which instead of underscoring set-pieces in the film were his own dramatisation of the characters, including 'Gemini', with whom Prince would have identified astrologically. It was a decision which, coupled to Prince's maverick reinterpretation of Batman/Bruce Wayne, the Joker and Vicki Vale, established the album as a separate creation, not just an OST. It's a relationship that somewhat parallels that between *Parade* and *Under The Cherry Moon*, except of course that *Batman* was a smash.

The opening track, 'The Future', is marked by one of Prince's most overt anti-drugs messages: take Ecstasy? 'I'd rather drink six razor blades from a paper cup.' A pop sentiment for a pop record. The chorus is astonishing and might have fitted on *Sign 'O' The Times*: 'Systematic overthrow of the underclass / Hollywood conjures images of the past / New world needs spirituality / That will last . . .', before repeating Batman's mantra about looking into a future that – in that time-honoured conclusion of Lincoln Steffens – 'works'. Ever since *Parade*, Prince had been obsessed with the relationship of past and future and the Gotham City created by Tim Burton, writers Sam Hamm and Warren Skaaren and their designers was the perfect blend of futurism and the 1940s neon retro glimpsed on the cover of *Sign 'O' The Times*. Prince spent some time on the set and wrote quickly: 'Electric Chair', the briskly upbeat 'Trust' and 'Partyman' for the Joker, 'The Arms of Orion' as a love duet for Bruce and Vicki (it was co-written with Sheena Easton, but wisely dropped from the soundtrack, as was the weak and sleazy rap 'Lemon Crush'), and 'Scandalous', written with John Nelson, for *Batman*. The movie's stars – Jack Nicholson, Michael Keaton and Kim Basinger – are guest 'presences' and Prince co-opts Jack's 'Don't dance with the devil in the pale moonlight' line as the pay-off to his longer than usual list of thanks.

All the cast characters come together on the concluding 'Batdance', which includes a brilliant part for the Sounds of Blackness Choir, a legendary St Paul outfit produced by Jimmy Jam and Terry Lewis and band-led by Levi Seacer after his departure from Prince. The track wasn't used on the soundtrack but it gave Prince his fourth number one hit and a fine video, directed by Albert Magnoli.

Despite a few other guest spots – engineer Femi Jiya and Anna Fantastic on 'Partyman', Matthew Larson on 'Batdance' – *Batman* was pretty much a solo Prince project, though he samples Bliss, Leeds, the choir and Clare Fischer's orchestral parts in his dense, swirling musical collage.

Elsewhere, the line-up was evolving. Sheila E moved on and was replaced by local Minneapolis drummer Michael Bland. There would also soon be a trio of male rappers, who featured strongly on the downbeat 'Nude' tour that introduced *Graffiti Bridge,* toughened up the female singing with the recruitment of Rosie Gaines and marked a switch from Prince's previous concept of rock-concert-as-sex-show. He hadn't yet completely tired of accessorising his entourage with talented blondes and called up Dutch saxophonist Candy Dulfer. Though she was featured on the 'Partyman' video, she declined to tour, perhaps unwilling to join Easton, Sheila, Susannah, Cat and the others in the roster of 'Prince's women', as *Rolling Stone* headlined a cover feature.

Their number was shortly to be increased when Basinger became a regular 'presence' in Prince's bed as well. More than most of his actual or putative girlfriends, the blonde actress seemed to fall completely under his spell, and seemingly believed that they would marry. He seemed equally infatuated with her; apparently $9^1/_2$ *Weeks*, in which she had starred opposite – or under – Mickey Rourke, was one of his favourite films. As well as paying off her make-up artist husband, Basinger fired her management and gave the account to Albert Magnoli, who had replaced Steve Fargnoli as Prince's representative on earth. There were rumours that Basinger's family were so concerned about the relationship and her new boyfriend's behaviour that they more or less kidnapped her back. 'Scandalous' had been Prince's love song to her – appropriately titled, given what the tabloids made of the relationship – and she contributed a few ecstatic groans to a twelve-inch version, an eighteen-minute 'suite' which includes some of his most turbulent, even angry guitar playing. Any further plans to encourage her singing career came to nought when the relationship foundered, though it did have a creative legacy in the shape of a draft movie script.

In the event, Candy Dulfer stuck around longer than Kim Basinger, long enough to record 'Release It' with The Time for the next album. It was to feature yet another cast, some new, some familiar, and given Prince's recent dabbling in film – and film stars – it was no surprise that it had a cinematic component.

12

In the final sequence of *Under the Cherry Moon* the words 'may U live 2 see the dawn' appear onscreen. Fans assumed that, James Bond fan as he is, Prince was announcing the next film in an unstoppable sequence. Most of the film critics who'd panned his directorial debut, and that means most film critics, prayed that it wasn't. Despite the panning, Prince wasn't yet done with the movies. His involvement in *Batman* had rekindled an enthusiasm, but *Graffiti Bridge*, released in 1990, wasn't the quick follow-up he might have wanted. Like its predecessors, it was both film and album. Like *Purple Rain*, it featured old friends, rivals and protégés. The same blessing, word for word, appears on the soundtrack album sleeve. The new dawn hadn't yet broken, it seemed.

At the cusp of a new decade, Prince was growing up, and growing a beard. One cynic suggested that he wanted to look like Jesus when he hit the age of thirty-three. On thephotographic evidence, he looks more like illusionist and endurance artist David Blaine. Unlike Blaine and contrary to his reputation as a driven loner, Prince wasn't solitary in

Paisley Park. *Graffiti Bridge* is similar to *Parade* in sounding more like a revue soundtrack than a rock album, and it's unique in the Prince canon in that it features other acts, albeit shaped and soundtracked by the director/auteur. Perhaps another of the tiny ice ages that swept across his creative personality from time to time was receding.

However, on a business level, Prince's career was drifting towards crisis. After parting company with Cavallo, Ruffalo and Fargnoli, he had hooked up for a time with Albert Magnoli, who, however improbable a relationship it seemed, might be said to have understood Prince's strengths and weaknesses better than anyone. Magnoli was tempted away, though, and after a brief period with Randy Phillips and Arnold Stiefel, Prince made the fateful decision to manage himself. Significantly, his nominal president was his old friend and security consultant Gilbert Davison, while the role of executive VP went to publicist Jill Willis. (Davison left Paisley Park in 1994 and bought out Prince's debt-laden Glam Slam club, renaming it Quest.) *Graffiti Bridge* was the first casualty of Magnoli's absence and the starkest sign that, when he had no one to butt ideas up against, even Prince's legendary creative judgement was flawed.

The original idea had been to create not so much a sequel to *Purple Rain* as a parallel line that told the story of The Time. Prince was concurrently working on the group's third album *Pandemonium*, for which, as Jamie Starr, he again wrote all the material, sharing a nominal credit on 'Jerk Out' with Morris Day, Jellybean Johnson and Terry Lewis.

No one knows how the original script, drafted with Basinger, was supposed to run, but the film that emerged was a drab vanity feature with the thinnest of storylines and in which The Time had only a secondary part. Prince did hint that Warner weren't interested in a Time biopic. At first, it seemed that an older and ever more sombre Prince might have abandoned the wobbly futurism of *Purple Rain* and the anachronistic fantasy of *Under the Cherry Moon* in favour of something more realistic, even literal – 'Graffiti Bridge' is, after all, a real location in Minneapolis, where the taggers hung out. The finished film inhabits neither a recognisable reality, nor an engrossing fantasy realm. It is virtually plotless, badly acted, and appallingly edited, despite the best efforts of Steve Rivkin, who was helicoptered in to save the project after the test screenings. Rivkin provides yet another sibling connection in the Prince story; he is the brother of long-time drummer Bobby Z and David Z from the early days. Neither he nor *de facto* director Peter McDonald could make much of a muddled and boring script, filmed and recorded at speed and in notably paranoid circumstances. *Graffiti Bridge* bombed in America; Europe only ever saw it on video.

With the departure of Basinger, Prince hastily rewrote the female lead and cast poet Ingrid Chavez, for whose debut album, *May 19, 1992*, he was also writing songs. The redoubtable Jill Jones was cast as his girlfriend and is one of the film's (very) few redeeming features. Its main problem isn't the result of haste so much as of seriously divided attention. Prince couldn't give the project the same hands-on approach that so incensed the professional cast of *Under the Cherry Moon* because he had too many other commitments bubbling under.

The soundtrack album reflects that rather more positively. As well as ten new Prince songs and three by The Time, there are cuts featuring P-Funk godfather George Clinton, whose mothership staging made an impact on Prince's concept for the later *Diamonds and Pearls* tour, and from new Paisley Park signings Tevin Campbell and Mavis Staples, whose appearance on the scene confirmed what later became obvious with the recruitment of Rosie Gaines: that Prince was tiring of merely decorative female singers and anxious to match his own growing confidence in normal register singing (less and less falsetto in evidence) with appropriately strong women's voices. Staples and Campbell take the lead on the title track, backed by Levi Seacer, Boni Boyer and Sheila E, and on a second version of 'New Power Generation', where T.C. Ellis and old friend Robin Power are also featured.

New Power Generation had started as a concept. It was now a song and was shortly to be the new group as well. Its first appearance on *Graffiti Bridge* is an interesting example of Prince looking backwards and forwards. The drummer is Morris Day, unexceptional in comparison to the peerless Sheila E or the funky Michael Bland, but adept enough and a link back to old times. Gaines is on hand to provide what's credited as 'vocal icing' (actually more substantial than that) and the other backing voices are the first acknowledged appearance of the NPG.

* * *

Most of the work was done at Paisley Park, with heavy input from engineer Martin Koppelman and some valuable troubleshooting by David Z. Campbell's 'Round And Round' was recorded at Electric Lady studios in New York and George Clinton's overdubs on 'We Can Funk' were FedExed in from Detroit. It might look as though Prince went back to a favourite studio, Sunset Sound in L.A., and the old engineering partnership of Susan Rogers and Coke Johnson for one of the album's two genuine classics, but 'Joy in Repetition' – pure, archetypal Prince genius – was actually a holdover from the abandoned *Crystal Ball* project. In some circumstances, using old tracks might be taken as a sign of current staleness, but Prince had an unfailing instinct for where a song might work and, besides, his rejects are generally better than most artists' best takes. 'Joy in Repetition' is where *Graffiti Bridge* takes off.

The album opens with 'Can't Stop This Feeling I Got', a workmanlike groove headed up by a sardonic spoken intro. 'New Power Generation', The Time's 'Release It' (featuring Candy Dulfer) and 'The Question of U' all follow before Prince delivers a quirky gem in 'Elephants & Flowers', one of the first tracks put down after the epic *Lovesexy* tour. However, along with the album's most successful single, the taut, asymmetrical 'Thieves in the Temple', it's 'Joy in Repetition' that stands out. Prince has rarely been more knowing, more self-referential, more allusive and more nakedly emotional in a single song. It also features one of his most unfettered guitar solos. The party clatter at the opening is a familiar enough Prince device, but coupled to the song's bluesy opening measures it's reminiscent of Miles Davis's *You're Under Arrest*, crossed with a Carlos Santana track. The Miles record is one of the anachronisms in *Under the Cherry Moon*, where it features prominently in one scene, but Prince's debt to the guitarist is confirmed by what sounds like a stalled reference to 'Soul Sacrifice'. The title 'Joy in Repetition' has an obvious erotic thrust, but it refers to the joys of music first and foremost. Its genius is to pare down hectic rhythm shifts, a complex vocal and a harmonically tense melody to a swaying, two-chord figure on the repeated words 'love me'. There are other agendas in the song – prayer, nostalgia, love as performance rather than intimacy, a strong sense of place and occasion – that suggest it's a very personal piece. It builds satisfyingly, somewhat in the manner of 'Purple Rain' and 'The Cross', but just as the storm subsides Prince cuts the track off dead with a soft giggle. It's a totally disarming moment.

'Thieves in the Temple' is an altogether simpler thing, a joggling three-chord phrase that builds, inverts and subsides on the hookline. Again, though, Prince plays games with bar-lengths and with the faintly Middle Eastern harmony. It's effortless songcraft, effortlessly delivered. It was one of only two songs from *Graffiti Bridge* – the other is 'The Question of U' – which Prince built into the regular set-list on the summer 1990 'Nude' tour of Japan and Europe. The highpoint of the itinerary was a nearly three-week residency at the Wembley Arena in London which, partly because with those few exceptions it was a greatest hits package, probably represents the post-*Purple Rain* highpoint of Prince's popularity in the UK. Perversely, some of those who had criticised previous tours for their burlesquerie and sexual excesses were dismissive of the new, toned-down version and male rapper-dancers. The tour name was deliberately provocative, and played on memories of past tours' states of undress and sexual antics but what was 'Nude' this time was the music, a deliberately stripped-down sound, tightly choreographed by Prince's enigmatic shouted instructions (oddly reminiscent of Duke Ellington). It was the closest anyone came to hearing *The Black Album* brought to live action.

The tour also brought to an end Prince's association with the long-serving Matt Fink and with guitarist Miko Weaver, both of whom decided to try for solo success (or suspected that halcyon days at Paisley Park were coming to an end). For the forthcoming sessions Levi Seacer was promoted to rhythm guitar, while 'childhood idol' Sonny 'T' Thompson (who can apparently 'play a French girl's measurements on the bass') takes care of the bottom end. Tommy Barbarella, no doubt recruited for his name – it was originally Elm – and now the one white face in the line-up, is put in charge of the trademarked Purpleaxe sampler. With Michael Bland on drums – and an unofficial moratorium on drum machines – the New Power Generation formula was complete.

The first indication of a new Prince album was a limited-edition giveaway single released to club DJs on June 7, 1991, Prince's thirty-second birthday. The track was 'Gett Off', a slice of dirty erotic funk laced with imaginative sexual analogies and the infamous 'twenty-three positions in a one-night stand' line. With *Diamonds and Pearls* Prince rediscovered how to make hit singles, three more aside from 'Gett Off', which became his most remixed track yet. It was also the single that Warner didn't want to put out, considering it too explicit. The promo for 'Cream' and the show Prince put together for the album tour showed some recognition that the sparser (and *pace* Rosie Gaines) maler line-up of the 'Nude' tour was a harder package to sell. He sidelined Tony M, Kirk Johnson and Damon Dickson and called up lookalikes Laurie Elle and Robia La Morte to play the notional roles of 'Diamond' and 'Pearl'. It's the latter who's mauled on the 'Gett Off' video and who's pictured having the eponymous goo licked suggestively off her fingers on 'Cream'. It was to be his most successful single for some time, but apart from breaking new audience regions, notably on a first tour to Australia, Prince seemed to be consolidating rather than moving forward.

Diamonds and Pearls isn't an album of retreads, but the group sound suggests a certain similarity to *Purple Rain*, even though the NPG is a palpably tighter and blacker outfit than

The Revolution. Having ceded some creative responsibility to group members and thus created the open, rock sound of his biggest selling album, Prince had now constructed a group so tightly marshalled that it sounded as though he were playing all the instruments himself. He had come full circle. Almost everyone who saw the NPG perform live commented on how rigorously rehearsed they looked, how very 'Prince' they sounded. And how very 'James Brown', who used to fine band members for getting a single note wrong. The habit of playing small-scale club dates after regular concerts gave Prince's personnel a chance to explore a more improvisatory side of the music, without the elaborate paraphernalia of the full show. For *Diamonds and Pearls* he went back to the big-budget spectacle of *Lovesexy*, but kept the critics interested with musicianly 'secret' gigs.

'Nude''s greatest hits format had underlined how substantial the Prince canon had become, but with it came a certain inertia of expectation that made it harder – chart hits notwithstanding – to break in new material. There's little on *Diamonds and Pearls* beyond the singles that would merit automatic inclusion on a 'best of' set – the title track, 'Cream' and 'Gett Off' are on different volumes of 1993's *The Hits* – but perhaps the most substantial track in terms of substance is 'Money Don't Matter 2 Night', apparently co-written with Rosie Gaines. Her style has always contained an element of social engagement and here she registers a protest, formulaic but sincere, about the first Gulf War. It's a solitary and mild protest gesture in an album dedicated to a new brand of melodic soul-funk, but it stands out sharply from the rest. Gaines is said to have had a torrid time with NPG, all but ostracised by the band and ignored by Prince. She did, however, remain an on–off member until 1996 and *Emancipation*. Her initial replacement was a young Hispanic called Mayte Garcia.

* * *

Given his productivity and given how long he'd been obsessively shapeshifting, changing direction, changing back, changing gender, no one could have grudged Prince a moment to mark time, put out a modest record, put on a good show. The problem was that *Diamonds and Pearls* came right before the most turbulent and difficult period of his life. Not only would he fall out terminally with his record company, but he would announce his own death and resurrection, not as Prince but as an unpronounceable astrological sign that would stump fans, interviewers, fellow-musicians, writers, editors, even his future wife for the next seven years.

13

When Mayte Janelle Garcia made her wedding vows on Valentine's Day 1996 she never once spoke her new husband's name. At the appropriate point in the ceremony – 'I, Mayte, take thee . . . to my lawful wedded husband' – she merely pointed to an unusually shaped gold pendant hanging round her neck. For the past two and a half years, the man she was marrying had refused to acknowledge his birth name and insisted on being identified only by an unpronounceable symbol.

It soon transpired that this was not just a simple, albeit eccentric, act of deed poll. Had Mayte been unwise enough to plight her troth to 'Prince', she would have found herself a widow *avant le fait*, for 'Prince' had died on his thirty-fifth birthday. His album *Come*, issued the following year, gave what appeared to be birth and death dates – half a biblical lifespan, 1958–1993 – and posed him in grainy black and white in front of what looked like a mausoleum. After that dark and brooding release, mostly reworked scratchings from the studio floor issued to fulfil his contract but by no means his least interesting record, the name Prince disappeared from his records for the better part of a decade. For the time being, bewildered journalists and editors learned to render his new 'name' in regular ASCII text as O(+>. Since the word from the man himself was that 'it doesn't pronounce, it just *is*', they got used to calling him The Artist Formerly Known as Prince, or TAFKAP.

One talk-show hostess, perhaps alert to the possibilities of rhyme, addressed him as 'Taffy'. A bantering concert crowd tried out 'Mr Nelson', which he acknowledged with a smile. Real fans tried to get by with 'Symbol'; sceptics dismissed him as 'Squiggle'; cynics took a double shot at his stature and petulant demeanour with 'Symbolina'; the truly desperate had little cards printed up with the emblem and held them aloft every time the sacred name was mentioned. One hopes that somewhere in his long, sour battle with the label that had fostered him and given him his creative freedom, ♀ found a moment to smile, even if only at all the free publicity.

* * *

The symbol itself made its first appearance on *Come*'s imme-diate predecessor, a 1992 album known variously as ♀ and *Love Symbol*. Its predecessor can be seen dangling from Prince's ear on the cover of *Graffiti Bridge* and standing in for the 't' in 'Graffiti'. In that form, it's basically a combi-nation of the astrological signs for male and female, an emblem of Prince's androgynous creative personae. He had apparently been experimenting with similar graphics since his teens, scribbled in the scruffy notebooks that are never far from his side. (This mania for sketching is something else he shared with Miles Davis, whose magic marker 'art' now commands thousands of dollars.) Some of his custom guitars were already made in unlikely shapes; a ⚲ version would soon follow. The new symbol adds just one element to the *Graffiti Bridge* version, giving it some of the characteristics of a crucifix and an *ankh*. Michael Bland's Egyptian-styled costumes – which made him resemble a charter member of the Sun Ra Arkestra – often incorporated the same device.

It's usually suggested that Prince's decision to change – or abandon – his name was a sudden one, a whim or a furious flounce at Warner's intransigence. It was, in fact, signalled some way ahead. The irony is that ⚲/*Love Symbol* begins with the most explicit declaration of his old identity yet. On 'My Name is Prince', he emulates a rap aesthetic drawn from graffiti in which 'putting your name up' is the essential component. Intriguingly, the new hip-hop was the one branch of black music which seemed to resist Prince's colonising urge. His rapping was never better than lame, and usually handed over to someone else in the NPG; it's Tony M who delivers the 'U must become a Prince before U're a king anyway' line. For all its vividly interlocked accompaniment, 'My Name is Prince' could seem like a dreary, repetitive chant, delivered in a throaty Springsteen bellow. Which may be an important clue. Just as there was endless debate about whether the redneck philosophy of *Born in the USA*, album and song, was genuinely felt or ironic, and whether Bruce was wrapping himself in the flag or subverting patriotism (answer: both, and very profitably), so it wasn't quite clear whether Prince expected this flagrant self-display to be taken seriously or to be seen as part of some witty sloughing of identity.

Once you accept there's a level of playful irony to the song, its boastful overkill – 'he ain't leaving this town till he's had your daughter, on the first day God made the sea but on the seventh he made *me*' – and its orgasmic yelps, male and female, its position on the album and in Prince's new agenda becomes more obvious. It's bracketed on the album with a song called 'The Sacrifice of Victor', which brings his old identity full circle. It's the journalist Vanessa Bartholomew's challenge to him to 'tell me the truth', looped and echoed, that cues up the song. In it, Prince seems to rehearse much of his youth and upbringing – violence at home, Bernadette Anderson, being bussed to school in 1967 – before setting his feet to the road that will lead him out of that past and see him re-emerge, like some Bunyanesque pilgrim, as 'Victor'. Other matters arising out of the song are more enigmatic: for instance, was Prince really 'epileptic till the age of seven'? On the lyric sheet, the word 'TRUE' is written in backward script at this point. The video to '7', which predicts a very different, more explicitly biblical apocalypse to the one described on *1999*, showed Prince and Mayte destroying his old selves. This is meant to be the prelude to a new identity (and the destruction of the seven killers who have destroyed the princess's father), but it's also very simply the kind of thing you do when you genuinely fall in love for the first time: throwing away the address book, the trinkets and gifts, old associations. ♀ may be a ritual of self-transformation, but, despite the fact that he is having phone sex with Kirstie Alley/Vanessa on the intro to 'The Sacrifice of Victor', the whole album, like *Emancipation* three years later, is an extended love song to Mayte.

* * *

And Mayte almost deserves a book of her own. Mayte Janelle Garcia (some sources give 'Jannell') was a military child, born in Puerto Rico on November 12, 1973, but fated by her father's postings to live life on the move. While he was stationed in Egypt, Mayte began to study belly dancing and became the world's youngest professional belly dancer at the age of sixteen. Later, in Germany, she added classical ballet to her repertoire, and it was there that the teenage Prince fan – apparently first attracted by the Arabic feel of 'Thieves in the Temple' – managed to smuggle a show-reel to her idol backstage. Prince apparently fell in love (not with the video of her dancing but with the photograph on the front) and claims to have told Rosie Gaines on the spot that this was the girl he was going to marry. Ironic, given that Mayte – no singer – would replace Gaines in the NPG and have more attention lavished by Prince on her *Children of the Sun* album than Gaines received on her *Closer than Close*. The cynical but realistic riposte is that Mayte's project needed all the help it could get.

Prince sent her a song and asked if she could choreograph it. She was hired before the next album was complete and it is her exotic features which look down from the clouds above the New Power Generation ('introducing Mayte') on the liner photograph to ♀. She also appears on the cover, standing with Prince in a futuristic cityscape, but ringed by ten little girls. They look like music counsellor and den mother from some nightmare summer camp. It's not clear whether Mayte, inspired by her brief sojourn in Egypt, first floated ideas of reincarnation, but if he didn't initiate it Prince very quickly bought into the idea, and the notion that he and Mayte were connected at some distant point in the past, as brother and sister – or as one and the same person, which he implies on 'And God Created Woman' – became the album's fantasy scenario and the basis of a new media spin.

As ever, Prince builds in a level of irony. When Vanessa Bartholomew takes his return call – voice and identity unconvincingly disguised as Victor – she's dismissive of his attempts to come on to her and makes it clear that if he doesn't give her a story, she'll simply make one up. If the rumours are true and the sixteen-year-old crown princess of Cairo has joined the New Power Generation then Vanessa is surely way too old, even for a 320-year-old avatar? (Mayte was actually eighteen but why get in the way of a good cradle-snatching storyline?) Vanessa's sarcastic debunking leaves the listener wondering whether the whole thing really is just a publicity stunt confected by the ever-knowing Prince. But then one remembers Alley's well-publicised commitment to Scientology, which hangs on an even more elaborate mythos, and Prince's knowingness takes on yet another dimension. As ever, he is 'a box, in a box, in a box'.

During their brief 'interview', Vanessa mentions his new 'opera'. Though later that year eleven Prince songs were built into an interactive musical theatre piece called *Ulysses*, premiered in August 1993 at his Glam Slam West club, the only track on ♀ that sounds remotely operatic is the preposterously overcooked '3 Chains o' Gold', a song with *Phantom of the Opera* pretensions that touches on love, loss, death and misunderstanding, and in turn sets up the album's bizarre identity-shifting climax.

* * *

Prince's apparent determination to go under a new name was reinforced by his collaboration with black-and-white photographer Terry Gydesen on a book called *The Sacrifice of Victor*. Concert crowds who shouted the name, though, got even shorter shrift than when they called him Prince. Some of the pictures appeared on the cover of *Come*. It was to be his last album as Prince until 2000 and was mainly reworked instrumentals from the vault, including some that had been aired in *Ulysses*. For nearly a decade and a half Prince had answered to the siren call of complete artistic independence and had found himself on the rocks; the one-eyed monster of profit-and-loss was catching up with him at last.

Relations with Warner had been strained since the enigmatic *Around the World in a Day* reversed what seemed to be an unstoppable market trend with what record executives considered the most perverse sequel in popular music history. After that, things went from bad to worse. After ♀, the label shut down the Paisley Park imprint and insisted that if Prince wanted to release 'The Most Beautiful Girl in the World', which he wrote the day after receiving the bad news from Warner, he would have to foot the bill himself. Perversely, it was a massive hit, and his first number one single in the UK. That hit convinced Prince that he could survive very well without Warner; they could release old stuff from the vault until they released him from his contract, while new songs would be aired in clubs and at concerts. He also established his own retail outlet, a mail order label known as 1-800-NEW-FUNK, and though contractually forbidden to record for any other label, it was widely – and understandably – believed that he was as much involved in NPG's 1994 *Gold Nigga* album as in his own official work and as he had been in Time and Family side-projects.

Warner were – equally understandably – determined to claw back some of their generous investment in an artist who threatened to become a liability. In 1993, they released two volumes of hits, which were also available as a double set with a bonus disc of B-sides. There were two new singles, 'Peach' and 'Pink Cashmere', which were the last new tracks he released as Prince; he regarded the *Hits/B-sides* issue as confirmation that his old performing self was dead. He was, however, still in contractual thrall to Warner and wouldn't be free of his contract until the summer of 1996 and the release of *Chaos and Disorder*, an album cobbled together with members of the (old) New Power Generation which returned disastrous sales, a mere 100,000 copies. By that time, he was officially known as ♀ or The Artist Formerly Known as Prince and had taken to writing the word SLAVE on his cheek in eyebrow pencil. It appears again as a song title on the joyous *Emancipation*, an album again devoted almost entirely to his love for Mayte: 'Friend, Lover, Sister, Mother/Wife'.

* * *

If there was a growing consensus about Prince's artistic 'decline' – and he even allowed Twin Cities journalist Jim Walsh to raise the issue in a liner note to 1995's *The Gold Experience* – it was almost entirely a tabloid creation. Though his fidelity was and remained questionable, settling down with Mayte, and later marrying her, robbed the press of a regular supply of scandalous Prince stories. Eccentric behaviour like swapping clothes with her and sending her onstage as 'Prince' – in line with his conviction that on some astral plane they were one and the same person – had begun to pall. There were few, if any, interviews, and even photo shoots, at which Prince always projected powerfully, were passing their sell-by date.

What the press – other than the hipper Minneapolis papers – didn't reflect was that Prince had never been more active. When he picked up a BMI award in London he muttered something about being perfectly free when he played a concert but 'on record – slave'. At home, he and his band were jamming at Paisley Park virtually every night, often following a small-scale date at one of his Glam Slam clubs. He was making as much music and with as much enthusiasm as ever. Just not for Warner. And, if a July 1993 statement was to be believed, he was shortly to retire from studio recording to explore other media: as well as an undented ambition to make movies, there was talk of writing musicals and ballet scores.

As queues for new Prince albums dwindled away, his loyal fans relied ever more on the red light of a Sony Pro glowing dimly through a club tablecloth; audience tapes and the occasional pressed-up vinyl bootleg became badges of solidarity with an embattled artist. Fortunately, both for his label and ultimately his own reputation, Prince's archive was so generously stocked with strong unreleased material that there should have been no need for the kind of sour contract-breaker, either deliberately perverse (like Lou Reed's now-canonised *Metal Machine Music*) or full of mawkish self-pity and insider references.

Though sympathies are usually reserved for the artist in cases of contractual dispute – creative David vs corporate Goliath – it is hard not to feel for Warner; or, more accurately, to feel for those former Warner senior executives, Russ Thyret, Larry Waronker (left end 1995), and ex-CEO Mo Ostin (left just before Christmas 1994) who had backed Prince to the hilt since 1977, dealt with his tantrums and eccentricities and then had to sit back and listen as he publically blackguarded their successors for . . . not doing what Prince wanted, basically. More galling still was that his enmity seemed to increase off American soil, where it was harder for Warner to respond in kind. During 1995, he gave a string of interviews to the British press which suggested that the company had long been out of touch with what 'the fans' wanted. Again, read, what Prince wanted.

The reality was that since the hasty *Around the World in a Day*, Prince's sales had plummeted and seemed to be in terminal decline. That record had been issued in the face of corporate misgivings and, ever since, Prince had consistently resisted Warner's tried-and-tested formula of just one album per year. He was already in debt to Warner; some said in the region of $15 million. Redeployed, his Warner budget could have launched two or three promising youngsters, like the teenage Tevin Campbell who'd featured on *Graffiti Bridge* or some of the artists Prince released on his *1-800-New Funk* compilation. The very fact that he was already acting as an independent while still obligated to Warner prompted discussions about legal action. Warner believed, not without warrant, that Prince had breached his contract by appearing alongside Mayte on the New Power Generation release *Exodus* and promoting the 'Get Wild' single – albeit pseudonymously and with a veil over his face – on a British television programme. The latest pseudonym had an ominous ring; by calling himself 'Tora Tora', was Prince conceding that he was on a kamikaze run, committing professional suicide?

Despite an August 1992 deal which provided $100 million for six albums (and included some development capital for Paisley Park), Prince was already deeply mired in financial problems. His Glam Slam chain folded and much of his merchandising went to the wall. With most of his management team long gone and his contact with the outside world intermittent at best, he continued to overspend, though to his credit most of the money went on making music rather than fast cars or cocaine. The tour to promote *The Gold Experience*, his last-but-one Warner record, long delayed by the label, was a naked effort to raise cash; ticket sales were slow. The label may have had irrevocable mandates on Prince's publishing to help offset the overdraft, and they also had a potentially lucrative back catalogue, but as far as new material was concerned it was unlikely that Warner was ever going to see a return on its money. Even at a notional $10 million per album, it seemed unlikely that Prince would, either.

The official name-change presented Warner with yet another, expensive problem. In order that press copy should

correctly identify their maverick artist as ♀, a special logo
had to be devised and sent out to newspapers and magazines on floppy disks. The company also put out a press
release aimed at laughing their recalcitrant star out of
countenance. Full of hearts, stars, dollar signs and smiley
faces, it basically said 'We don't care what our stars call
themselves but for God's sake, just to keep the peace, do
us a favour and don't call him Prince, eh?'

* * *

With an air of losses being cut, *The Black Album* was
released commercially in 1994, just after the rain-soaked
'memorial album' *Come*. Of the two, *Come* is unquestionably the more dangerous, in subject matter if not in
treatment. Though it features one intriguing experiment,
'Solo', co-written with David Henry Hwang, its musical
material consists largely of found riffs and accompaniments
from the Paisley Park archive, reworked with new vocal
lines. Though not credited to the NPG, it features essentially the same line-up as ♀, but now minus Levi Seacer
and with Morris 'Mr' Hayes on keyboards, and an array
of guest horns. 'Horny' is probably the right word to
describe both the musical arrangements and the overall tone.
With the Warner situation all but terminal, Prince saw no
need to hold back and this last album as himself is an
extended and explicit seduction, punctuated by murmured
invitations to 'come'. The title track runs to a sleazy eleven

minutes, with Prince going through his usual half-amused, half-threatening cajole. The brief final track, 'Orgasm', is a wry confirmation of the guitar-as-phallus cliché, an unhinged and distorted solo over a girl's ecstatic moaning; the 'vocal' credit merely reads 'She knows'.

'Papa' gives domestic violence a surreal edge, almost as if Prince had been reading Peter Reich's *The Book of Dreams*, and its air of menace saves it from bathos. The terse titles – 'Space', 'Pheromone', 'Loose!', 'Race', 'Dark', 'Letitgo' – exactly reflect the record's spare arrangements and offhand delivery. They also reflect Prince's determination not to give Warner anything remotely resembling a chart single; he'd proved to his own satisfaction with 'The Most Beautiful Girl in the World' that he could turn those out overnight, if needed.

A brilliant, instinctive pastiche of Philly soul, it was the outstanding track on *The Gold Experience*, which was eventually released in 1995. Warner's decision to delay the record had been what prompted Prince to write SLAVE on his cheek. By then, of course, he was no longer Prince and it was two years before he made his debut as ♀. The oddity of *Come* was that it appeared under the old name, though given that the back-story was Prince's 'death', this made a certain sense. *The Gold Experience* has a loose storyline as well, though not one that anyone remembers and the between-track passages are no more than an awkward armature for another effortless but also cheerless synthesis of pop, rock, funk, jazz, gospel and soul. 'Dolphin' is as unalloyed a pop song as he'd written since 'Alphabet St', while 'Endorphinmachine' suggested that he still hadn't given up on distorted guitar rock.

The following year's *Chaos and Disorder* took that side a step further on 'I Rock, Therefore I Am' and the heavy 'I Like It Here', but otherwise worked a familiar seam (the jazz-funk of 'Dig U Better Dead', the near-perfect pop of 'Dinner with Delores'), with just a few magpie-ish forays into hip-hop, ragga and other contemporary beats. Prince's standard reaction to the suggestion that the Minneapolis sound had been overtaken by hip-hop was, predictably, that he'd done it first. It was just that he could actually *sing*. As ever, though, he was a brilliant, instantaneous assimilator, pulling together influences in real time, counterpunching challenges to his dominance, improvising new wrinkles on a vast body of black American music.

For the moment, though, he was something other than an agile thief. Though some pointed out that SLAVE was also the word used for copying machines in recording studios and thus possibly a hint to would-be bootleggers out there, there was a disturbing irony in seeing a light-skinned black man, who for a time commanded a market presence equalled only by Madonna and Michael Jackson, publically declaring his enslavement to the system. Film director Spike Lee, who had crossed paths with Prince at various points, asked him why he only seemed to work with white girls. Prince's tricksterish answer was that that only applied to the 'successful' stuff; the implication being that, as on *Under the Cherry Moon*, he'd play the exotic to knock the starch out of whitey, but that he knew where his real loyalties and his real audience lay. He also seemed naively disturbed that while Cassius Clay's transformation into Muhammad Ali, or O'Shea Jackson into Ice Cube, were all accepted as political gestures, the transformation of Prince Rogers Nelson into ♀ was dismissed as publicity.

Having declared his enslavement, Prince could only recover his credibility with an Emancipation Proclamation.

14

On May 16, 2000 Prince reverted to his original name. In the past, such announcements had acquired a mystical significance by being made on his birthday. On this occasion, the circumstances were more pragmatic. That was the day his publishing contract with Warner-Chappell finally ran out; Prince's songs were his own again. It was a bittersweet return since the same month marked the end of his marriage to Mayte Nelson. The internet buzzed with rumours about the reason for the breakdown – his infidelity, her infidelity, the failure of her career (thousands of copies of her *Children of the Sun* album lay boxed and unsold in the warehouse) – but the bruising effects of tabloid speculation, to say nothing of the very public birth and death of baby Gregory, can't be underestimated. Prince's optimistic, offhand prediction that there would be other children hadn't come to pass. The utopian family predicted on the cover of the ♀ album had given way to a spotlit loneliness.

Years of cancelled gigs, abortive interviews and pointlessly enigmatic appearances had alienated all but a hard core of fans. His 1999 record *Rave Un2 The Joy Fantastic* was a familiar blend of styles, all effortlessly delivered but lacklustre as a package and without a single defining track. Significantly, the album was remembered for guest spots from rapper Chuck D, harmonica and harmony vocals from Sheryl Crow (whose own songwriting style owed something to both Prince and *his* mentor Joni Mitchell) and No Doubt's Gwen Stefani (a fine duet on 'So Far, So Pleased').

As far as the record-buying public was concerned – those who still visited stores rather than surfing the fast-developing internet or hip to Prince's mail-order set-up – Prince hadn't made a convincing record for three years; 1998's *New Power Soul* was a lightweight, meat-free flop. For those who kept abreast with 1-800-New-Funk and with his www.love4oneanother.com website, that same year had also yielded *The Truth*, a mostly acoustic album, and a final appearance of the three-CD *Crystal Ball*, a grab-bag of mostly older material whose title piece was a brooding, almost depressive song originally slated for *Sign 'O' The Times*, but apparently vetoed by Warner. Prince also found room for 'Cloreenbaconskin', which he had written with Morris Day for The Time, the stunningly good 'Days of Wild', and 'Dream Factory', one of several songs from this period which take sideswipes at the chemical and emotional perils of rock stardom (i.e. swipes at Michael Jackson). There is left-over material from *Parade* ('Sexual Suicide' and 'An Honest Man') and from the *Ulysses* project. *The Truth* also included some gems, but more importantly it represented an artist growing up in public, prepared to be serious, prepared to be nostalgic (as he is on 'Circle of Amour'), and prepared to let the songs themselves do most of the work; the title cut is just Prince, guitar and a few keyboard flourishes, and it's electrifying. The abiding impression was once again amazement at how much material – new, old, reworked – Prince could command.

These records did eventually make an appearance in record stores, but for the most part they were subscription releases, not pressed until orders had passed a break-even point. Many of the tracks had circulated as bootlegs for years, but by 1998 Prince had once again an overground presence and major-label backing. Clive Davis of Arista had in a previous incarnation at Columbia been an important supporter of the often ill-served Miles Davis; ironically, when Miles left behind his Columbia contract, he spent his last few years with Warner. There was a further irony in that Prince had campaigned fiercely for singer Toni Braxton and earlier for TLC in their money battles with LaFace Records, a subsidiary of Arista. Clive Davis's reward was *Rave Un2 The Joy Fantastic* and the knowledge that more Prince product was circulating by other means than by straight retail sales. His artist's frequent proclamations about karma must had an uncomfortable resonance.

There had been an earlier saviour. In 1996 Charles Koppelman signed Prince to EMI Capitol and gave him leave to release a triple album. Not *Crystal Ball*, but every bit as significant in Prince's effort to free himself from creative slavery.

* * *

Fans and critics awaited the release of *Emancipation* with the understandable conviction that were it anything other than a major statement, Prince/♀ could be judged to have suffered a technical knock-out. EMI presumably waited for the tapes with similar trepidation. Prince's website confirmed that this was a lifetime project, its three discs modelled on the building of the pyramids and thus aligned with the star-fields overhead. Songs like 'Da, Da, Da', 'Friend, Lover, Sister, Mother/Wife' (written for his wedding reception), 'Slave', all suggested that this was a record with a strong autobiographical slant. So, too, did references to Mayte's expected baby and the sound of his foetal heartbeat on 'Sex in the Summer', originally entitled 'Conception'. Mayte's swelling belly – overprinted with music staves, just to show that Prince considered both conceptions of equal importance – is built into the surreal anthropomorphic landscape of the liner booklet, along with a poignant collage of black-and-white family photographs. The presence of a rare cover version, the Stylistics' 'Betcha by Golly Wow!', suggested strongly that more than ever Prince wanted to inscribe himself on the history of black American music. He would later tour with former Sly Stone bassist Larry Graham and members of Graham

Central Station, and play Sly's very Prince-like 'Thank You (Falettinme Be Mice Elf Agin)'.

That might have been a more appropriate cover version for the *Emancipation* set list, except that the publishing shackles would not fall away for another few years and that for the time being he was still ♀ and not Prince. It was obvious, though, from the party sounds and tightly knit beats of the opening 'Jam of the Year' that whatever he was called, he was still very much the same artist who had started out nearly two decades earlier with a new synthesis of funk.

Impending fatherhood and a fat cuttings-book whose contents ranged from hyperbole to vitriol were the most obvious reminders that here was an artist approaching the age of forty. The official back catalogue, greatest hits anthologies and bootleg compilations were a reminder of how the intervening years had been filled. But what becomes increasingly obvious on *Emancipation* is that, fresh directions like *Parade* and *Sign 'O' The Times* apart, and efforts to merge black r'n'b and white pop-rock aside, Prince did not so much 'develop' as steadily unfold a single coherent vision which depends on a deep and instinctive understanding of a whole continuum of black American music and *its* often problematic, sometimes antagonistic continuities with the cultural mainstream. For all his *Zeitgeist*-checking flourishes – a hint of ragga on *Chaos and Disorder*, a foray into techno on *Emancipation*'s 'The Computer' (a guest vocal by Kate Bush) – Prince is interested in a music that is beyond fashion and that might last as long as Giza.

He has been pop's most successful tomb-raider, an innovator only technically. His early use of synthesizers and Linn drums was pragmatic rather than central to his vision. As soon as he made contact with musicians able to convey his ideas in real-time, or who could be moulded to his needs, he ceded reponsibility to them. Though at times the backing musicians seemed little more than set-dressing, though he has often ruthlessly colonised ideas for which others claimed legitimate credit, and though after The Revolution and New Power Generation he once again declared himself onlie begetter of his records, Prince has always had a profound need of others. His almost obsessive need for approbation goes beyond vanity (and beyond Vanity, that toy-box, puppetmaster phase when he treated people as means rather than ends) and stands ultimately as the downside of his intense spiritual engagement.

Prince is as ever teasingly unspecific in terms of actual religion – he appears in the liner booklet as what can only be described as a Franciscan Hindu dervish, in modified cassock and wearing a *bindhi* mark on his brow. So personal a statement, it belongs to him alone. Like *Lovesexy* before it, and in a more obviously secular way *Sign 'O' The Times*, *Emancipation* is a spiritual testament. What makes it different is that in marriage to Mayte, and in the imminent prospect of bringing forth a child, Prince objictified his long-standing male/female dichotomy – misleading to call him androgynous – and his compulsion to produce. The sheer physicality of his musical conception was never limited to doing the splits and backflips on stage. It also had something to do with the actual means of production, laying hands on guitars, drums, keyboards, all the instruments he could actually play. When he made fluid jet from the neck of his guitar he was obviously bent on titillating, as he was when he French-kissed and dry-humped female members of the band, but he was also unconsciously striving for a kind of creative *jouissance* that went beyond the usual highs, lows, fads and formulae of popular music performance.

* * *

Marked by the passage of time though it is, distorted by excessive expectation, warped by spite and wilful misreading, *Emancipation* is arguably Prince's most impressive achievement. It is far from being his best album, but it is certainly not just an act of megalomania, nor a posthumous monument. The Egyptological metaphor – which surfaces again on 'Muse 2 The Pharaoh', one of the best tracks on 2001's *The Rainbow Children* – was widely taken as a further sign of battiness, some Isis/Osiris nonsense cooked up with his belly-dancing sister/wife, but in its three-hour span the album itself provides a convincing foundation for it.

Listening to *Emancipation* straight through is a considerable undertaking because almost every song is both a deliberate reminder of past styles and experiments, and at the same time offers an earnest view of what might yet be to come. Where *Sign 'O' The Times* married a new social awareness to deceptively lightweight pop within a free-flowing jazz setting, where *The Black Album* rode a hard, cold riff from beginning to end, *Emancipation* has a coherence of tone and structure that seems entirely at odds with its disparate means. Great albums are always more than mere sequences of great songs. Really great albums – *Revolver*, *Pet Sounds*, *'Automatic' For The People*, *OK Computer* – are rarely more than a dozen to fifteen tracks in length. *Emancipation* has thirty-seven.

Among them, there are flaring inconsistencies. 'White Mansion' and 'Damned If 👁 Do' have much of the self-pity that broke through on *Chaos and Disorder*, but then 'Slave' turns Prince's private woes into a chilling field blues which for all its reference to the Warner dispute has a universal resonance. Other inconsistencies seem more ironic. Appended to the cheerful 'Joint 2 Joint' is a safe-sex warning to wear a condom; the very next track is 'The Holy River', and the next again 'Let's Have a Baby'. Mayte was apparently moved that Prince had furnished his mansion with a crib, even before they met. In a characteristic shapeshift he suggests that seeing it turns her on, pushes the button marked PLAY. Such glimpses of the former, supposedly unregenerate Prince surface throughout – 'Sleep Around', 'Face Down' – but the emotional temper of these songs is never what the listener is led to expect and their place in the sequence always implies other agendas.

Three enormous slabs of music that gather into their own secret chambers much of the work that has occupied him for the last two decades. The difference between Prince and the pyramid builders is, again, that he is also the thief. These treasure-houses are wilfully despoiled even before they are sealed off in the final mix. Their sound is deliberately left ragged in places. There is the usual irruption of un-explained sound, abrupt cuts, mid-bar edits. The transcendence is always kept at a human level. For all the promise of 'The Cross' or 'Saviour' here, Prince's next world is always a new version of this world, expressed in music.

* * *

In his mid-forties, he lives more quietly, dresses more soberly, and was rumoured to have married again, to twenty-five-year-old Paisley Park employee Manuela Testolini in a secret ceremony conducted in Hawaii on New Year's Eve 2001. Neither he nor Mani have confirmed or denied the story, nor whether the ritual reflected Prince's rumoured conver-sion to the Jehovah's Witnesses.

He continues to work and to perform, again more quietly and soberly, but steadily consolidating the audience lost in the dark years of the 1990s. Almost inevitably, when set against the paradigm-shifting work of *Dirty Mind, Purple Rain* and *Sign 'O' The Times*, or against the sheer bulk and symbolic potency of *Emancipation*, recent work has seemed low-key, even muted. Released in 2001, *The Rainbow Children* saw Prince working with a new band – including Larry Graham and with only Morris Hayes surviving from past line-ups – and offering a gentle hint as to how he has found happiness with Mani: 'She Loves Me 4 Me'. The following year's *N.E.W.S.* saw a further personnel change, but also the return of the loyal Eric Leeds, and a project that contained further references to the New World Edition of the Bible, and sparked more rumours that Prince might have thrown in his lot with the Witnesses. Then, in 2004, the quiet, competent *Musicology*, which has to be the wryest, most telling title of his entire twenty-five-year span.

Prince is arguably the most important popular musican of his time. He is responsible for no single, identifiable stylistic development, but yet remains entirely *sui generis*. His private life, temperament, height, sexual orientation, religious affiliation have all been pored over as obsessively as his music, and yet it is the musicologists rather than the gossip columnists, sexual therapists, cult leaders or Moral Majoritarians who will pronounce the final word on his life and career. If those two threads are not so tightly inter-wound as to defy separation. Prince lives to make music and vice versa. It is his essence, a reverential kleptomania that seems incapable of being satiated but which arranges its booty in constantly fascinating forms.

Emancipation freed him but confirmed his enslavement to a complex muse. The years after robbed him of a wife and son, of his mother and the father who played such a powerful and ambiguous part in his development. Never before has Prince's future seemed more open. The only guarantee? 'A new song every day, for the rest of my life.'

Afterword

The Prince story is not over, but its dramas and its innovations now seem locked in an unexpectedly distant past. To some extent the rise of hip-hop culture ended Prince's creative reign in much the same way as it finally demonstrated the finite nature of Miles Davis's creative flexibility. Though both musicians borrowed elements of it – Prince with more conviction – these were little more than staying gestures in the face of the inevitable. Though few of them shared his ecstatic utopianism, Prince and the rappers were more thoroughly divided by a broad shift in black music towards live improvisation while Prince, for all his extravagant live acts, remained essentially a studio artist, crafting his music in layers and textures. Recorded rap is a curiously unsatisfactory phenomenon and, for all the myriad 'rap' parts on records in other genres, only uneasily assimilable to pop, soul and jazz recording.

It might be argued that Prince simply waited out a phase in American music when his distinctive values were not widely appreciated and then quietly returned to prominence after the millennium, restored to his original identity and still able to create exciting pop/soul/funk. He draws on a vast back catalogue of material, committed to paper, to Sony Pro tapes and to hard drives over nearly thirty years and there is no reason to believe that he will not continue to do so. It is exactly that long since *For You* signalled the arrival of a bright new star on the American scene. The enigma of Prince is how little stylistic impact he has made relative to the length and success of his career. There is no obvious 'school' of Prince, no obvious line of descent and while one occasionally hears an artist or group who has tried to reproduce that chiming, insistent rhythm guitar, bassless mix and chunky electronic percussion, these are mostly decorative rather than structural devices, in the same way that Prince's borrowing from hip-hop was rarely structural.

As he approaches fifty Prince both covets and rejects senior artist status. He is wise enough to have evolved slowly away from earlier personas, styles and image without ever leaving them entirely behind. No more Ziggy Stardust moments for him. He retains just enough of his old subversive edge to suggest that he is still capable of surprise and, ironically, just enough to remind us that it was all a carefully donned disguise in the first place.

Prince's story, even in its darkest moments, is one of estimable control, a career devoted to specific musical and creative ends with entire concentration and with few significant distractions. Around him, there has grown a substantial mythology, much of which he now – fatherless, motherless, married again – quietly ignores. Most of it was smoke and mirrors, crumbs and trails for the media, who gleefully accepted every new twist in the story, thought they had Prince firmly in pocket – sometimes in the cross-hairs – and only wakened up late, as he began again to count his money, to the awareness that they had never had him after all . . .

2006

Discography

Notes

* = as Prince and The Revolution

\# = as Prince and New Power Generation

\#\# = as New Power Generation only

♀ = as ♀

Albums

[Album (Label, first release date – approx. worldwide sales (rounded) – US/UK chart position)]

For You (Warner Bros, October 1978 – <500,000 – 163/–)

Prince (Warner Bros, October 1979 – 2,000,000 – 22/–)

Dirty Mind (Warner Bros, October 1980 – 1,500,000 – 45/–)

Controversy (Warner Bros, November 1981 – 2,500,000 – 21/–)

1999 (* 2 LP, Warner Bros, February 1983 – 6,000,000 – 9/30)

Purple Rain (* Warner Bros, August 1984 – 20,000,000 – 1/7)

Around the World in a Day (* Paisley Park, 1985 – 4,500,000 – 1/5)

Parade (Warner Bros, May 1986 – >4,000,000 – 3/4)

[*Crystal Ball* (Warner Bros, 1986/7 – withdrawn)]

Sign 'O' The Times (2 LP, Warner Bros, March 1987 – 4,000,000 – 6/4)

The Black Album (scheduled Warner Bros, November 1987; finally released Paisley Park, September 1994 – >1,000,000 – 47/36)

Lovesexy (Paisley Park, February 1988 – <3,000,000 – 11/1)

Batman (Paisley Park, June 1989 – <5,000,000 – 1/1)

Graffiti Bridge (Paisley Park, August 1990 – >2,000,000 – 6/1)

Diamonds and Pearls (# Paisley Park, October 1991 – 6,500,000 – 3/2)

♀ (# Paisley Park, October 1992 – >2,500,000 – 5/1)

Goldnigga (## Paisley Park, 1993 – n/a)

Come (Paisley Park, August 1994 – 15/1)

The Gold Experience (♀ Warner Bros/NPG, October 1995 – <1,500,000 – 6/4)

Exodus (## Paisley Park, 1995 – n/a)

Chaos and Disorder (♀ Warner Bros, July 1996 – <1,500,000 – 26/14)

Emancipation (♀ 3 CD, EMI/NPG, November 1996 – 2,000,000 – 11/18)

New Power Soul (## NPG, June 1998 – n/a – 22/–)

Rave Un2 The Joy Fantastic (♀ Arista/NPG, November 1999 – 1,750,000 – 18/–)

The Rainbow Children (Redline, November 2001 – >850,000 – 109/–)

N.E.W.S. (instrumental NPG/Big Daddy, July 2003)

Musicology (Columbia/NPG, April 2004 – >6,250,000 – 3/3)

3121 (Universal, March 2006 – 3,000,000 – 1/9)

Through NPG Music Club only:

Rave Un2 The Joy Fantastic (♀)

One Nite Alone . . . Live! (December 2002 – 700,000)

C-Note (downloadable – 2003)

Prince

Xpectation (instrumental – downloadable – 2003)
The Chocolate Invasion (downloadable – 2004)
The Slaughterhouse (downloadable – 2004)

Compilations and outtakes:
Dirty Mind/Controversy (cassette compilation of albums, 1981)
The Hits 1 (Warner Bros, September 1993 – >3,000,000 – 46/5)
The Hits 2 (Warner Bros, September 1993 – <3,500,000 – 54/5)
The Hits/The B Sides (3 CD Warner Bros, September 1993 – >1,500,00 – 19/4)
1800 NEW FUNK (Prince songs by other acts on NPG, 1994)
Crystal Ball (⚥ 3 CD outtakes, NPG, March 1998 – 1,000,000 – 62/–; also see above for withdrawn album of same name)
Royal Box (import only box set, March 1999)
The Vault: Old Friends 4 Sale (ouch! Warner Bros, August 1999 – n/a – 85/–)
The Very Best of Prince (Rhino, July 2001 – >2,500,000 – 55/2)
Ultimate (Rhino/WEA, March 2006 – n/a – 61/24)

Others:
The Beautiful Experience (⚥ EP, 1994)
Girl 6 (soundtrack – Warner Bros, 1996 – n/a – 75/–)
One Man Jam (teenage Prince with Pepe Willie/94 East, issued on Recall, August 2002)

Selected singles
[album (label – date)
'single' (US Billboard/r 'n' b/dance/UK chart positions)]
from:
For You (WB – 1978)
'Soft and Wet' (92/12/–/–)
'Just as Long as We're Together' (–/91/–/–)

Prince (WB – 1979)
'I Wanna Be Your Lover' (11/1/2/41)
'Why You Wanna Treat Me So Bad' (–/13/–/–)
'Still Waiting' (–/65/–/–)
'Sexy Dancer' (–/–/2/–)

Dirty Mind (WB – 1980)
'Uptown' (101/5/5–)
'Dirty Mind' (–/65/5/–)
'Do It All NIght' (–/–/–/–)

Controversy (1981)
'Controversy' (70/3/1/– reissue 1993, UK 5)
'Let's Work' (104/9/1/–)
'Do Me, Baby' (–/–/–/–)

1999 (1982)
'1999' (12/4/1/25 – reissued 1998 & 1999 – highest UK 10)
'Little Red Corvette' (6/15/61/54 – reissued 1989 with '1999', UK 92)
'Delirious' (8/18/–/–)
'Let's Pretend We're Married' (52/55/52/–)

Purple Rain (1984)
'When Doves Cry' (**1/1/1/4**)
'Let's Go Crazy' (**1/1/1/7**)
'Purple Rain' (2/4/–/8)
'I Would Die 4 U' (8/11/50/58)

Around the World in a Day (1985)
'Paisley Park' (–/–/–/18)
'Raspberry Beret' (2/3/4/25)
'Pop Life' (7/8/5/60)

Parade (1986)
'Kiss' (**1/1/1/6** – reissued 1988, UK 76)
'Mountains' (23/15/11/–)
'Anotherloverholenyohead' (63/18/21/36)
'Girls & Boys' (–/–/31/11)

Sign 'O' The Times (1987)
'Sign 'O' The Times' (3/1//2/10)
'If I Was Your Girlfriend' (67/12/–/20)
'U Got The Look' (with Sheena Easton: 2/11/–/11)
'I Could Never Take The Place Of Your Man' (10/14/4/29)
'Hot Thing' (63/14/4/–)

Lovesexy (1988)
'Alphabet St.' (8/3/22/9)
'Glam Slam' (–/44/–/29)
'I Wish You Heaven' (–/18/–/24)

Batman (1989)
'Batdance' (**1/1/1/2**)
'Partyman' (18/5/45/14)
'The Arms of Orion' (with Sheena Easton – 36/–/–/27)
'Scandalous' (–/5/–/–)

Graffiti Bridge (1990)
'Thieves in the Temple' (6/1/9/7)
'New Power Generation' (64/27/–/26)

Diamonds and Pearls (1991)
'Gett Off' (21/6/1/4)
'Cream' (**1**/–/–/15)
'Diamonds and Pearls' (3/1/–/25)

♀ (1992)
'Sexy MF/Strollin' (66/76/–/4)
'My Name Is Prince' (36/25/9/7 – remix UK 51)
'7' (7!/61/–/27)

The Hits/B Sides (1993)
'Pink Cashmere' (50/14/–/–)
{'Peach' (107/14/–/–)
{'Nothing Compares 2 U' (–/62/–/–)

The Beautiful Experience (1994)
'The Most Beautiful Girl in The World' (3/2/–/1)

Come (1994)
'Letitgo' (31/10/–/–)
'Space' (–/71/–/–)

The Gold Experience (1995)
'👁 Hate U' (12/3/–/20)
'Gold' (88/92/–/10)

Emancipation (1996)
'Betcha By Golly Wow' (31/10/–/11)
'The Holy River' (58/–/–/19)

Rave Un2 The Joy Fantastic (1999)
'The Greatest Romance Ever Sold' (63/23/–/–)

Musicology (2004)
'Musicology' (120/44/–/–)
'Cinnamon Girl' (–/–/–/43)

3121 (2006)
'Black Sweat' (60/82/–/43)

Selected songs written for or covered+ by other artists:
Stevie Nicks, 'Stand Back' (1983, US 5)
+Chaka Khan, 'I Feel For You' (1984, US 3, UK 1)
Sheila E, 'The Glamorous Life' (1984, US 7)
    'The Belle Of St Mark' (1985, US 34, UK 18)
    'A Love Bizarre' (1986, US 11)
Sheena Easton, 'Sugar Walls' (1985, US 9)
The Bangles, 'Manic Monday' (1986, US 2, UK 2)
+Art of Noise/Tom Jones, 'Kiss' (1988, UK 8)
+Sinead O'Connor, 'Nothing Compares 2 U' (1990, US 1, UK 1)
Kid Creole and the Coconuts, 'The Sex of It' (1990, UK 29)
Tevin Campbell, 'Round and Round' (1991, US 11)
Martika, 'Love . . . Thy Will Be Done' (1991, US 10, UK 9)
    'Martika's Kitchen' (1991, UK 17)
Monie Love, 'Born 2 B.R.E.E.D' (1993, UK 18)
    'In A Word or 2/The Power' (1993, UK 33)
+Ginuwine, 'When Doves Cry' (1997, UK 10)
+Jordan Knight, 'I Could Never Take the Place of Your Man' (1999, US 31)
+Alicia Keys, 'How Come You Don't Call Me' (2002, UK 26)
+Inaya Day, 'Nasty Girl' (2005, UK 9)
plus material for The Time, The Family, Masarati, Apollonia 6, Vanity 6, Mayte and New Power Generation . . .

Selected songs written by Prince and recorded by others:
Paula Abdul, 'U'; Deborah Allen, 'Telepathy'; Ingrid Chavez, 'Elephant Box'; Candy Dulfer, 'Sunday Afternoon'; Nona Hendryx, 'Baby Go-Go'; Jill Jones, 'For Love'; Lois Lane, 'Qualified'; Dale Bozzio, 'So Strong'; George Clinton, 'The Big Pump'; Joe Cocker,

'Five Women'; Andre Cymone, 'The Dance Electric'; Ed DeBarge, 'Tip O' My Tongue'; Eric Leeds, 'Times Squared'; Kenny Rogers, 'You're My Love'; Earth, Wind & Fire, 'Super Hero'; Graham Central Station, 'Utopia'.

Selected video and DVD:
Purple Rain (video/DVD, Warner, 1984/2004)
Prince and the Revolution: Live (video, Warner, 1985)
Graffiti Bridge (video, Warner Bros, 1990)
Sign 'O' The Times (video/DVD, MCA/WEA, 1991/2003)
Gett Off (video, Warner Bros, 1991)
Diamonds and Pearls (video, Rhino/WEA, 1992)
Hits Collection (video/DVD, Warner Bros, 1993/1999)
Rave Un2 The Year 2000 (video/DVD, Image Entertainment, 2000)
Live at the Aladdin, Las Vegas (DVD, Hip-O, 2003)

Index

Brian Morton

names 18–19, 169–70, 171, 181–2, 186
  aliases 20 (*see also under those names*)
nicknames 20, 39–40
Oedipal complex 14, 20, 22 , 90
paranoia xii, 117, 118
personas 16, 19–20, 45, 63, 75, 118, 197
politics 71, 110, 130
public relations 88–9, 176, 185, 198
reincarnation 16, 169, 170, 175
relations with father 20, 21–4, 25, 26, 50
relations with men 83, 99–100
relations with women 99–100, 117
  band members 83, 102, 103
  feminist 4, 104, 105, 138
  Lesbians 58, 84
  white girls 184–5
religious beliefs 75, 94, 113, 191
retire/decline x, 116, 144
rude boy icon 66, 70
sales xi, 178, 179, 180, 197–206
sex, love and God 71, 81, 94, 114, 150
sexual ambiguity 84, 100, 144, 172, 191
slave motif xi, 13, 178, 183, 184
tours 6, 17, 39, 65, 66, 140
  'Nude' 158, 166, 167
  Rick James 66, 67, 68, 79
  Rolling Stones 66, 67
  album tours *see under album titles*
  see also Prince/gigs
Prince Rogers Trio 18
Prince: A Pop Life 16, 35–6, 46
'Private Joy' (song) 72
PRN 109
Purple Rain (album) 73, 77, 94–8, 117, 119, 199
  autobiographical 19, 21, 59
  film 3, 6–7, 16, 24, 89–94
  tour 3, 39, 112, 116
'Purple Rain' (song) 54, 58, 95, 97, 202
'Question of U, The' (song) 164, 166
'Race' (song) 183
racism 32–3, 34, 35–6, 81, 82
radio stations 35, 52, 66, 81, 82
Rainbow Children, The (album) xi, 113, 192, 194
rap 148, 153, 172, 184, 196
'Raspberry Beret' (song/video) 8, 115, 153, 202
'Rave Un2 The Joy Fantastic' (song) 156
Rave Un2 The Joy Fantastic (album) 187, 188, 200
Red Shoes, The album (Kate Bush) 109
'Release It' (song) 159, 164
Revolution (band) 4, 67, 79, 82, 112, 118, 123, 140, 168, 191, 199, 206
  disbanded 116, 117, 130, 146
Richards, Keith 146
Rivkin, Bobby (Bobby Z) 43, 50–1, 92
Rivkin, David 43, 44, 50
Rivkin, Steve 43, 162
'Rock Hard in a Funky Place' (song) 148
Rogers, Susan (engineer) 135, 142–3, 164
Rolling Stones 64, 66, 74

'Ronnie, Talk to Russia' (song) 70
'Round and Round' (song) 164, 205
Rushen, Patrice 57
Sacrifice of Victor, The (book) 176
'Sacrifice of Victor, The' (song) 14, 19, 26, 32, 34, 173
Santana, Carlos 5, 52–3
'Saviour' (song) 194
'Scandalous' (song) 23, 157, 158, 203
Seacer, Levi 152, 157, 163, 166, 182
segregation, racial 32–3, 35–6, 81, 82
Sevelle, Taja 109
'Sex in the Summer' (song) 189
'Sexual suicide' (song) 187
'Sexy Dancer' (song) 57, 202
Sgt Pepper's Lonely Hearts Club Band 116
Shaw, Mattie (Prince's mother) 17–18, 21–2, 24–25, 27, 38, 39, 42
'She Loves Me 4 Me' (song) 195
'She Loves You' (Beatles) 56
Sheila E 100, 102–3, 143, 152, 157, 163, 205
  album contributions 123, 138, 147, 152, 153
Sign 'O' The Times (album) 8, 101, 128–31, 133–41, 145, 192–3, 200, 203
  sales 143, 200
  tour 140, 152
Sinatra, Frank 88
'Sister' (song) 69
'Slave' (song) 178, 189, 193
'Sleep Around' (song) 193
'Slow Love' (song) 137
Sly Stone 6, 38, 52, 55, 72, 76, 146
SMiLE album (Beach Boys) 129, 142
Smith, Charles 41
'So Blue' (song) 54
'So Far, So Pleased' (song) 187
'Soft and Wet' (song) 47, 52, 53, 66, 201
'Solo' (song) 182
'Sometimes It Snows In April' (song) 125
'Soul Sacrifice' (Miles Davis) 165
Sounds of Blackness Choir (band) 157
'Space' (song) 183, 204
Spooky Electric (Prince alias) 20, 150–1
Springsteen, Bruce 117, 172–3
'Stand Back' (song) 209, 205
Staples, Mavis 109, 163
'Starfish and Coffee' (song) 8, 137
Starr, Jamie (Prince alias) 20, 62, 70, 161
Stefani, Gwen 187
'Still Waiting' (song) 58, 202
Stipe, Michael 126
Stone City Band 67
Stone, Sly see Sly Stone
Straight And Smooth (Billy Lyle) 38
'Strange Relationship' (song) 101, 139
'Sugar Walls' (song) 102, 104, 205
Sunset Sound studio, LA 131, 164
'Supercalifragifunkysexy' (song) 147
'Take Me With U' (song) 94, 96
'Tambourine' (song) 114
Taylor, Don 65
Teena Marie (band) 79
'Temptation' (song) 113–14

Testolini, Manuela 194, 195
'Thank You (Falettinme Be Mice Elf Agin)' 7, 190
There's a Riot Going On album (Sly Stone) 146
'Thieves in the Temple' (song) 165, 174, 203
Thompson, Sonny 'T' 166
Thriller (Michael Jackson) 7, 8, 85
Thyret, Russ (Warners) 50, 54, 180
Time, The (band) 39, 69, 79, 85, 159, 164, 187
  albums 73, 107, 161
  Graffiti Bridge 91, 161, 162
Tony M 167, 172
Tora Tora (Prince alias) 20, 181
Tracy, Christopher (Prince alias) 20, 106, 120, 121
'Trust' (song) 157
Truth, The album 143, 187, 188
Tutu album (Miles Davis) 108
'U Got The Look' (song) 26, 101, 135, 137, 203
Ulysses (musical theatre) 176, 177, 187
Under the Cherry Moon (movie) 24, 49, 91, 120–3, 156, 160, 162, 163, 165, 184
'Under the Cherry Moon' (song) 23, 123
Uptown 72, 87, 111
'Uptown' (song) 63, 68, 69, 202
USA For Africa album 131
Vanity/Vanity 6 67, 68, 79, 83, 85, 100
'Venus De Milo' (song) 125
Vicari, Tommy 46, 50
Victor (Prince alias) 20, 173, 175
Warhol, Andy 40
Warner Brothers 14, 120, 155, 188
  censorship 62, 167
  marketing Prince 54, 56, 63, 64–5, 69, 141, 143
  Paisley Park imprint 111, 141, 177
  Prince contract 9, 13, 24, 50, 52, 177–8, 179, 180–1, 186
  Prince name change 19, 181–2
Waronker, Larry (Warners) 62, 80
'We Can Funk' (song) 164
Weaver, Miko (rhythm guitarist) 123, 152, 166
'When 2 R In Love' (song) 148, 154
'When Doves Cry' (song/video) 55, 97–8, 202, 205
'When We're Dancing Close and Slow' (song) 57
'When You Were Mine' (song) 68
White Album (Beatles) 115, 148
'White Mansion' (song) 193
'Why Should I Love You?' (song) 109
'Why You Wanna Treat Me So Bad'(song) 58, 202
Wild Heart, The album (Stevie Nicks) 109
Willie, Pepe (Linster) 42, 43–4, 49, 68
Wonder, Stevie xii, 6, 8, 47
You're Under Arrest (Miles Davis) 165
Z, Bobby 50–1, 61, 92, 162
Z, David 162, 164

210